ESCAPE FROM BERLIN

by

STEPHEN BLACK

Gotham Books

30 N Gould St.
Ste. 20820, Sheridan, WY 82801
https://gothambooksinc.com/

Phone: 1 (307) 464-7800

© 2023 *Stephen Black*. All rights reserved.

No part of this book may be reproduced, stored in a retrieval system, or transmitted by any means without the written permission of the author.

Published by Gotham Books (December 16, 2023)

ISBN: 979-8-88775-767-4 (P)
ISBN: 979-8-88775-768-1 (E)

Because of the dynamic nature of the Internet, any web addresses or links contained in this book may have changed since publication and may no longer be valid.

The views expressed in this work are solely those of the author and do not necessarily reflect the views of the publisher, and the publisher hereby disclaims any responsibility for them.

Content

Chapter One 1
Chapter Two 3
Chapter Three 7
Chapter Four 11
Chapter Five 15
Chapter Six... 17
Chapter Seven 19
Chapter Eight 25
Chapter Nine 31
Chapter Ten 33
Chapter Eleven 37
Chapter Twelve 43
Chapter Thirteen 45
Chapter Fourteen 53
Chapter Fifteen... 63
Chapter Sixteen.. 67
Chapter Seventeen 83
Chapter Eighteen.. 85
Chapter Nineteen 89
Chapter Twenty 93
Chapter Twenty-One 97
Chapter Twenty-Two... 101
Chapter Twenty-Three 103
Chapter Twenty-Four 105
Chapter Twenty-Five... 109
Chapter Twenty-Six 113

CHAPTER ONE

It is early 1939. The winds of war are creeping into the mindset of all of Europe and creating major concerns around the World. Adolph Hitler was appointed chancellor of Germany in January 1933 and has transformed the country into a single party dictatorship under the autocratic ideology of Nazism. Even with the rearmament of Germany there were many skeptics in the United States that whatever was going on in Europe was nothing that we should concern ourselves with.

In addition the civil war in Spain had just ended in 1939 in favor of the dictatorship of Generalissimo Franco. As time passed on a sinister relationship became a reality between Franco and Hitler which eventually created a major problem for all of Europe. To make things more unsettled there arose in Italy a change that was instigated by the rhetoric of the new leader Benito Mussolini that created the 3rd dictatorship on the Continent.

Two people, husband and wife, are trapped in a foreign country not speaking the language and losing their only contact, a tour guide, amidst some of the greatest political upheaval and turmoil in history. Then, being separated from each other in their attempt to find a route to safety and one that was not too well conceived in their haste. This is their story.

CHAPTER TWO

It was in the late summer of 1939, Pat and Chris Casey's children, Sam and Laura were preparing to go college in a few weeks. Chris was going to begin his sophomore class at Yale and Laura was to begin her freshman year at Sarah Lawrence. The autumn leaves would soon be turning into dramatic colors of red, yellow and orange. To those who live in the northeastern states consider this time of year to be the most beautiful. Both of the kids were very bright and were among the most popular in their circle of friends and were probably the best looking and were considered to be among the best looking. You could tell that they had mixed emotions about going back to school. They had a wonderful summer away at camp spending those days out of doors swimming, hiking, athletic competition of all kinds and of course the inevitable summer loves. They had formed some new friendships and had also reaffirmed some old relationships from years past at the same camp. The camp that they attended, first as campers and later on as counselors, was located in among the beautiful Adirondack Mountains. The camp was run by the owners of one of the most noted food catering companies on the East coast. Thus, the meals were wonderful at the camp and they would miss the wonderful meals. It wasn't that their Mom was not a good cook but the new foods that they were introduced to made mealtime at camp somewhat of an adventure.

Leaving the camp at the end of the summer, as in every summer, and returning to their normal environment at home and at school, did not come easily for Sam and Laura. The difficulty, as for many kids their age, centered around the new relationships they made that summer and their relationships they had at home during the school year. What about their boyfriend and girlfriend that they had not seen for several months since the end of the school year? Would there be a change in those relationships either due to the new relationships they had formed at camp or had the old relationships faded during the summer? The two months of carefree time at the summer camp was ended and they were going back to the hum drum predictable life at school. Both of them have worked as counselors at camp a number of years and, at the end of camp, the parents would tip them for watching over their kids during the summer and keeping them safe. So, both Sam and Laura were able to pocket a good deal of cash at the summer's end.

Everything was scheduled for school including the time they would arrive and the courses of study they would be taking. The school life for Laura as a freshman would be a new experience but not so for Sam. In addition both of the kids were athletic one playing football, baseball and running track (of course that would be Sam) and for Laura her love of being on the soccer field and her trying to make the school's team as a freshman. Sam, knowing that he would have to compete again to make the teams, he was feeling a goodly amount of anxiety. Had they improved, skill wise, over the summer or has someone on their respective teams beat them out and take away their chances of being on the teams.

Of course Pat and Chris could empathize with them in looking back at their teen age years, they were faced with the same anxieties as is true for most teenagers. Both of them had active social lives in high school and at college and they were voted as the most attractive couple in their senior year in high school. So, the apples did not fall very far from the tree. They had experienced some of the same concerns when they were at their children's ages but, since they were a couple while at both high school and college, there was no relationship problems to deal with. Sam and Laura were not much help to the kids in sharing their experience in relationships so that Laura and Sam would have to deal with this on their own. Chris and Pat did not look forward to the potential angst their children were possibly about to face as they dealt with both old and new relationships.

Pat and Chris took advantage of the time that the kids were away as they did each summer in the past. This really did not change much over the past few years they had been married. Pat was still the prettiest 40 year old in their social circle and Chris was still the athletic type having worked hard to stay fit by running, biking and playing tennis.

Chris had been on the track team in college and had lettered all four years. So, it was easy to see how Sam got involved in track and cross country as Chris became a coach of sorts. They did not have to worry about the kids interrupting a sexual event over the two months in the summer they were away. They really believed that their sex life was much more pleasurable during the summer. Chris felt comfortable walking around in the nude after showering hoping that it would turn Pat on to the possibility of having sex. Sometimes that worked but she caught on rather quickly to his motives and in reality the sex was no more than usual but it was more relaxed and was more freelance and more enjoyable while the kids were away.

Sure they had missed the kids during the summer so they were happy having them back with them back in their home before going off to school. Every summer that the kids were away Chris and Pat talked about the ways in which the kids might change in height, weight and maturity. There is no question that even though it is only for 2 months the changes are perceptible when the summer is over mostly for the better. Chris talked about when he came home from summer camp he did not think about how he might have changed but certainly he wanted to see if his parents had become more" with it" over the summer. As for most teenagers they thought that parents had not a bit of common sense and were "old fashioned" and not up the current trends. No doubt Sam and Laura felt the same way. Since Pat and Chris were sweethearts in high school and at college, their parents were good friends and socialized with each other and remain the very best friends.

In looking back on his teen years Chris viewed most adults and certainly his parents as a bunch of " old fuddy duddies" who had not a clue about things that were important to him. His Dad was a Vice President of a well known bank and his Mom taught school at a grade school nearby. It was obvious that both Pat and Chris were brought up in families that lived by their faith and God was ever present. Both families went to church on a regular basis and Sam and Laura were involved in several youth groups at their church. Chris served a term on the Vestry and Pat was very involved in the Women of the Church. The Episcopal Church they were members of very much looked like a small Anglican Church might look like in England. Much of the families social time revolved around Christ Church and its 300 or so communicants. As an adult, looking back on his growing up years, Chris realized that much of what his parents tried to teach him was right on target. Isn't that funny? We tend to be more respectful of our parents as we grow into maturity. Parents grow older and are not able to do many of the things that they were able to do when they were younger. Their children have a reversal of roles in that they become parents to their parents. Just as our parents were there for us as small children, we tend to treat our older parents as children that require our looking after them- a sort of reversal of caring. Both Pat and Chris had experienced this when their parents had grown old and needed their support. Both lost their parents in recent years. These losses became more of a downer for Sam and Laura as they were very close to their grandparents. Of course, Pat and Chris were not at an age of having to depend on their kids but that would change down the road.

CHAPTER THREE

Over the past 10 or 12 years it seemed that the world around them has changed dramatically. They had suffered through a rather severe recession beginning in the late '20s. Pat and Chris had graduated from college in 1920-21 when World War I was ending. They had met in high school and dated exclusively during those years and, when Pat graduated from college in 1921, they were married on the day of her graduation. Chris had graduated one year earlier with a degree in finance and had been given an opportunity to work for a major financial institution as an Economic Analyst. Having joined the firm right out of college his income was very modest being barely able to support himself. His parents helped out from time to time which was very much appreciated. Chris had taken an apartment with a good friend Mike so it helped with the rent. He could have stayed with his folks in order to save up some money since he and Pat planned to marry after her graduation. Pat received a degree in Education so that she could teach in Elementary School upon graduation.

In planning their lives after marriage they needed to decide where they could live mainly based on their income. They chose to live in a rather modest size town in New Jersey, mainly because Pat was offered a job at a local school teaching 3rd grade in walking distance from where they lived and Chris commuted to Wall Street everyday by train. Although their income was rather modest, they were able to make a down payment on a house. Chris had been living in an apartment with a roommate sharing in the rent. Of course his roommate Mike was not happy at his moving out but Mike understood and said he would find someone else to share in the rent. The fact was that after Chris moved out Mike and his girlfriend Carol decided to marry within a year. The two couples continued their friendship after their marriages.

As the early years of the 20's went by things were good for Chris and Pat. Chris got to benefit from the growth in the economy and he received promotion after promotion at the Bank he worked for. The Bank was so successful that one of the major banks in New York City took them over. Since by that time Chris had made significant contributions to his bank, the parent company (after the takeover) asked him to join them at their main location in New York City to head up the research part of the Bank. His new job was located down the street so there was little to no change in his goings and comings. At this time the stock markets were going great guns and the part that research played became more and more important to the investing public both for individual investors and for institutional investors. Chris's bank was one of the leading banking institutions and, as many of the banks' clients relied more and more on using Chris's research to help them in making investment decisions, he was becoming more and more valuable.

Chris and Pat moved to a larger home in the area where they were living as his income afforded them this opportunity. Their children were growing both in age and in maturity and they needed a larger house. Chris's income had been given a huge boost and it no longer became necessary for Pat to work so she became a stay home Mom and was doing a great job in raising the kids and in being a supper homemaker. She also found the time to become more involved at Christ Church and found the time to get involved in community affairs which also impacted their social life. It was a great time for their family. The kids were involved in sports in the community which eventually led to a major involvement at their high school. The only negative was in finding the time to get the kids to and from games, meets and practices. Kids in New Jersey could drive at age 16 so both Sam and Laura eventually were gifted with cars so they could be more mobile and relieve Chris and Laura with car pooling.

Chris commuted to his office on Pine Street right in the heart of Wall Street. He took the Erie Lackawanna to Hoboken and then a bus to a few blocks from his office. His success in business came at somewhat of a cost to his family. He would leave to go to work most days before his family got up and many days did not get home until after dark. Thus the time to spend with his family was shortened because of his work schedule sometimes out of town visiting some of his clients and researching Corporations that Chris covered for the Banks research department. He even had to work some on weekends as major changes developed that would impact Corporations and the economy. Chris had to bring his clients up to date on what he was forecasting both on the short term and long term in the economy and for specific industries.. So much of the bank's reputation was dependent on Chris's ability to be right more often than not. By the end of 1928 Chris had been given the title of Senior Vice President of the bank with a big increase in salary. Things continued to spiral up for his family as his income continued to increase while his responsibilities grew. All seemed to be well for Chris and his family.

By 1928 their kids were now 7 and 8 both going to the best private schools in the area. Families of means sent their kids to private schools as the classes would be smaller, the teachers more capable all to the end of a better education. It was also believed at that time children graduating from a prestigious private school they would have a better opportunity to be accepted to one of the premier Universities. As a family they had grown into the typical Banking family and had adjusted to this new way of life. The environment they lived and worked in was very competitive both in business, school for the kids and for Pat it was an extremely competitive social life. So many of the heads of family who lived in their neighborhood worked on Wall Street either for Investment Banks or for Commercial Banks so it would be obvious that their social life revolved around these families. Chris had spent almost all of his working life being aware of the competitive environment that he worked in. The ups and downs of the stock market created a good deal of personnel changes at the banking institutions and so in that way Chris was vulnerable. It was somewhat more difficult for Pat and the kids to make the adjustment from more or less a laid back lifestyle to what was called for due to Chris's position at the Bank as part of the Wall Street way of life. They struggled from time to time but in the end they made the adjustment. The upward mobility for the family to the upper echelon of Wall Street was a good road to be on. After Chris's promotion, it was evident that he was on a fast track. The chance for him to become CEO of the Bank in the near future was rumored all throughout the Bank. Life had been good to Chris and his family and the future looked even brighter.

CHAPTER FOUR

In the summer of 1929 there were warning signs that the great economic road that the United States had been on since the end of the war, was beginning to look suspect. There were cracks in the stability of some major banking institutions. At the time many noted economists were concerned with the effect of the decision by the Federal Reserve to contract the money supply and by the decision by the British to return to the Gold Standard at pre World War I parities.

Some argued that the failure on the part of free markets and a failure of government efforts to regulate interest rates might lead to a major recession. What was thought to be an ordinary recession, turned out to be The Great Depression. Not only was the United States affected but the entire world suffered some more than others. On September 4th,1929 stock prices began to fall and then on October 29,1929, better known as Black Tuesday, the stock market crashed and the news spread rapidly around the world. This crash on the US markets became a domino effect on markets around the world and thus the Great Depression took flight. The effects were devastating everywhere. Personal income, tax revenues, profits and prices dropped and international trade dropped by more than 50%. In the US unemployment rose to above 25%, with higher readings abroad. Those countries that were overly dependent on heavy industry suffered the worst and new construction came to an abrupt halt. Crop prices fell and thus the farming community was in dire straits. Cash cropping, mining and logging were adversely impacted and led to a major increase in unemployment as there were few alternative jobs.

The country was in chaos and the White House was unable to remedy this ongoing disaster. Heads of State around the world communicated without coming up with a fix that would work. Over the next several years , on balance, the world markets were in shambles. Many major players in the financial markets tried to create a sense of optimism such as John D. Rockefeller who said "These are the days when many are discouraged. In the 93 years of my life, depressions have come and gone. Prosperity has always returned and will again." In mid 1930 the market was able to rally back to the levels of the early part of 1929 which was still 30% lower than the peak in 1929.

This period and beyond, reaching into the mid to late decade of the 30's, took its toll on the Banking industry. Massive bank failures were a direct result of this Great Depression. Of course the effect on Chris's family was enormous. During several meetings of the Board of Directors it was decided that extreme personnel cuts had to be made if the Bank was to survive. All of the senior management folks had to take major cuts in their salaries and the days of huge bonuses were a thing of the past. Chris and his family they were visibly concerned and anxious about the future. Their family life would change dramatically going forward and they were forced to make some serious decisions on how to allocate their assets. They had to take their kids out of private school and have them enter the Public Schools in their area. It was hard for the kids, ages 9 and 10, to understand what was happening and think they suffered more than Pat and Chris did.

This change in lifestyle for the family required some hard choices but they tried and were successful in keeping the kids on an even keel. The Country Club was out of the question as were the many social functions they were used to attending. The fact of the matter was that many of their friends and neighbors were in the same fix so there was company to commiserate with. Finally it became necessary for Pat to seek employment as a teacher again and that source of income became a life saver. There seemed to be no end in sight. Thank goodness Chris had his job and because of the importance of his role at the Bank he was able to be a great asset to the health of his client base and to be a greater asset to the Bank. His standing in the Investment Community was uplifted because of his opinions regarding solutions that might be viable going forward. He was asked to attend a meeting in Washington to provide President Hoover and the Secretary of the Treasury with his take on possible solutions to the fear that was gripping not only the United States but all over the world. It is funny now to recall those meetings and some of Chris's ideas that they rejected by Hoover were important steps that FDR's administration embraced after his election. Chris welcomed the opportunity to provide the Government with his thoughts on how they might be able to overcome the tragedy that the world was focusing on. His thoughts mainly revolved around the idea that Governments had to greatly increase spending to get people back to work. Hoover rejected this idea because he did not believe in the Government getting too involved in the economy. Chris opined that public works programs would be ideal in getting folks back to work.

CHAPTER FIVE

At the height of the Depression noted British economist John Maynard Keynes voiced" To keep people fully employed governments have to run deficits when the economy has slowed as the private sector would not invest enough to keep production at normal levels. Governments should be called on during periods of economic crisis to pick up the slack by increasing government spending and cutting taxes.". His comments clearly affirmed what Chris Casey had told President Hoover but he never listened and was voted out of office in 1931.

As the Depression wore on in 1932 FDR won the White House mainly because the Republican administration under Herbert Hoover was blamed for the dire straits of the economy. In order to attack the Depression FDR tried Public Works, farm subsidies and other methods to jumpstart the economy. While this use of Government Funds did support somewhat of an economic recovery the country was never able to balance the budget. FDR , according to the Keynesians doctrine, made the valiant attempt to reverse the Depression. All of that changed when the United States entered WWII.

Many economists blame the sharp decline in international trade. The Taft-Hawley Tariff Act in 1930 which had a major influence in worsening the depression by almost bringing to a halt international trade. Taxes on imports to the US went from almost 26% to 50% from 1931 to 1935. American Exports dropped from about $5.2 billion to $1.7 billion in 1933. Hardest hit were farm products which caused many American farmers to default on their loans leading to the collapse of many small rural banks.

Leverage, due to the unheard of 10% margin requirements, was a major factor in the stock market crash in 1929. Investors were unable to meet the margin calls that were generated and thus the brokers called in these loans which could never be paid back. Banks began to fail as debtors defaulted on their loans and bank depositors attempted to take out their deposits which led to multiple bank runs. Failures of banks led to losses of billions of dollars in assets. A total of over 9000 banks failed during the decade of the 1930's. Bankers called in the loans which borrowers were not able to pay. Because of these bad loans the banks pulled back on their lending which created a major slowdown in money that might have been used to jump start the economy. This vicious cycle led to the downward acceleration of the economy. This process turned the 1930 recession into the Great Depression.

In most countries the recovery from the Depression began in 1933. The US did not get back to the 1929 GNP for over a decade. In 1940, prior to the start of WWII, the unemployment rate dropped to about 15% from the high of 25% in 1933. The policies of the FDR administration did accelerate the recovery but not enough to bring the country out of the Depression. The overriding point of view at this time was that the Great Depression ended when the United States entered WWII. It is true that the rearming policies in Europe helped stimulate those economies into the latter part of the 1930's. The fact is the entry into the war by the US did eliminate the effects of the Great Depression and unemployment dropped to 10% in 1941. Huge war spending doubled economic growth rates.

CHAPTER SIX

The decade of the 30's were most unsettling for Chris's family. The good news was that with Pat going to work as a school teacher the income problems were eased. In addition because of Chris's research and forecasting which were accurate, his position at the Bank was strong at the end of the decade. There was a great chance that in the near future he would assume the position of President and CEO. His dreams were close to coming true. Since things were going his way and it looked as if the Great Depression might be winding down, Pat and he planned to take a escorted bus trip in Germany in the spring of 1939. Since the US was not directly involved in the war in Europe they felt they would be safe on such a trip. There appeared to be a window for this trip which would not interfere with his work at the Bank. In all probability, he would be elected CEO and President by the Board prior to this trip. The timing would be perfect; come back from this vacation and assume his new role. In addition both of their kids would be going away to college with Sam a sophomore at Yale with a business major and Laura at Sarah Lawrence as a freshman.

The trip that they planned to visit Germany in 1939 became a reality and they were not the least bit concerned about their safety so long as other countries such as Great Britain and France did not enter the war.

Adolph Hitler was born in Austria in 1889. He was a decorated veteran of WWI. In 1921 he became the leader of the National Socialist German Workers Party. He was imprisoned for one year after his failed coup to take over the German Government. While in prison, he wrote his memoir Mein Kamph(My Struggle). Upon his release from prison he gained widespread support by promoting Pan-Germanism and anti-Semitism with his oratory and strategic use of propaganda. He was made Chancellor of the Third Reich in 1933, a dictatorship based on his values and ideology.

His New Order of absolute Nazi rule in Europe led to a pursuit of a policy of seizing land(living space) for the Aryan people which culminated in the invasion of Poland in 1939. In late 1939 the United Kingdom and France declared war on Germany as they had promised if Poland was invaded. Thus began WWII in Europe. The United States basically stood on the side lines except providing the Allies equipment and money to fight the Germans. This laze faire position of the US lasted until 1941 when the US declared war on the Axis Powers-Japan and Germany and Italy.

The trip that they planned to visit Germany in 1939 became a reality and they were not the least bit concerned about their safety so long as other countries such as Great Britain and France did not enter the war. It was late in August that Chris and Pat prepared for the overseas trip. Neither one of them had been to the Continent and they were looking forward to the trip. Shortly before leaving on the trip the Board of Directors, upon the retirement of the long term CEO, John A. Edwards, voted unanimously for Chris to be President and CEO. The transition would take place in mid September. Chris knew that when he returned after their trip he would have to step right into the job.

CHAPTER SEVEN

With great anticipation Pat and Chris boarded a Pan American flight in New York that would take them non stop to London where they would change planes and land in Berlin several hours later. Neither of them had ever been on a plane as large as the Super G Constellation. It had four engines and accommodated over 200 passengers. Since the flight would take 8 to 9 hours to get to London, they would be served dinner and then try to get some sleep while crossing the Atlantic. Dinner was just ok but they ordered wine with dinner. They hoped that the wine would relax them and allow them to sleep some. They slept fitfully but the trip seemed to take not as long as they expected. They landed in London at 8:30 in the morning and were quickly transferred by bus to another plane waiting to fly them to Berlin. Within a few hours they arrived at their final destination. They were met at the gate by a representative of the Tour group who helped gather their luggage and then proceeded to their hotel by taxi.

The hotel they would be staying at was the Prinz-Albrecht-Strasse. On the way there they could not help but notice all the billboards and signs adorned with the German Swastika. Also there seemed to be a great number men, women and children dressed in what appeared to be military uniforms.

The hotel was one of great elegance and grandeur. They were escorted to the reception desk where they were greeted by a representative of the hotel dressed in a dark business suit with a starched collar. Very impressive they thought. Looking around there were several pictures of Adolph Hitler on the walls and several bronze busts of Hitler and some others they did not recognize.

After being shown to their room they were advised that the tour group would meet for cocktails in the hall next to the main dining room at 7PM. At that time they would join the other members of the tour which would take them to the high spots in Germany. There were cocktails and hoerdervs for the group to snack on while the leader of the Tour company gave them an outline of what they might expect. Interestingly enough Pat and Chris were the only Americans on the trip with folks from all over Europe mainly from Spain, Portugal and France. The tour leader introduced himself as Herr Hans Ulbricht. He asked that during the tour each day those who were seated in the outside seat needed to move to a seat behind the next morning so as to meet others on the tour. When they board the bus the next morning they should not sit with their spouse or traveling partner. He continued on to say that he was a native Berliner and had lived here his entire life.

They retired early after a rather unimpressive dinner at the hotel. Having not been exposed to German cuisine before they found the food somewhat distasteful but they decided that things would improve as the 10 day trip wore on.

They awoke early to have breakfast with the others on the trip and then they would be taken on a bus ride around in Berlin to see the sights that were promised in the travel brochure. Regarding breakfast, it was somewhat better than last nights dinner as they were served a few different kinds of sausage and some kinds of cheese with fruits and pastries. They were looking forward to the start of the bus trip so they all hurried through the breakfast. They noticed that some of the tour group put pastries in napkins and placed them in their pockets or purses apparently to eat mid morning so Pat did the same.

Upon boarding the bus Chris sat next to a elderly woman whose name tag said she was from Belgium. Pat was seated next to a middle aged gentleman whose name tag said he was from Spain. Chris thought to himself "What a good looking man and how well dressed" He overheard him talking to Pat in English but Chris was not as lucky as the woman seated next to him did not speak or understand English.

Chris noticed that the street the bus was on was very crowded and the street sign said Wilhelm-Strasse. The tour guide pointed out the massive headquarters of Herr Goring, the new Air Ministry building, the home of the German Luftwaffe. Going on a bit further they made a right turn onto a beautiful street that was guarded on both sides by a magnificent array of trees. The street sign said Unter Der Linden.

The bus finally made a stop. Hans told them that this was the Olympic Stadium host to the 1936 Olympics. One would certainly notice as they went along on this journey that Hans Ulbricht, their guide, had been thoroughly indoctrinated in the message that Adolf Hitler and the country of Germany were trying to portray to the world. They saw military units drilling openly and the Luftwaffe was on display in many airfields. They saw buses with machine gun mounts on their roofs. As they were arriving at the Olympic Stadium, Hans began his message about the history of the Stadium and of the Olympics that were held here.

"On August 1, 1936 the Olympics were officially inaugurated by the head of state, Adolf Hitler. The lighting of the Olympic torch began in Amsterdam in 1928. However the torch for the 1936 Olympiad began its marathon journey from Greece and then through Bulgaria, Yugoslavia, Hungary, Czechoslovakia, Austria and then Germany. This idea for the tour of the torch was the idea of our minister Joseph Goebbels as a means of bringing the message of the true Germany to Europe. Amazingly all records were broken attendance wise as 4 million tickets were sold for all the events."

As they left the bus at the Olympic Stadium they saw Nazi banners papered over everything. Many of the men and young children they saw were wearing what looked like some type of military uniforms that they had seen before on the streets of Berlin. Their guide continued his tale of that Olympiad " Another little know fact was that it was the first Olympiad that was televised with 25 giant screens all over Berlin so that our people could be in awe of the work done by our Chancellor, Adolph Hitler, and to the greatness of the Third Reich." It was obvious to all of them that these comments were all part of the propaganda that was all around them everywhere they went in Berlin. Both Pat and Chris were somewhat upset that there was no mention of the most famous athlete of the games, an American Negro, Jesse Owens. He won gold medals in track in the 100, 200 meter runs, the long jump, and was a member of the 4x100 relay team that won the gold medal. The Olympic Stadium was apparently was still being used for athletic events. They were all impressed by the size of the stadium and how well it was being kept up and manicured as was most of Berlin.

After this visit they returned to the bus where Hans provided refreshments of coffee and hot chocolate and strudel (the famous pastry of Germany). No question that all of this consideration and hospitality was meant to impress them about the new Germany, The Third Reich.

One of the major events that was being hosted by the City of Berlin was the 1939 Berlin Auto and Motorcycle Show. It was billed as an international event. This show was being held in 9 huge exhibit halls adjacent to Berlin's Witzleben train station at the Kaiserdam/Funkturm exhibit grounds. Hans told them that so far tens of thousands of visitors from around the world came to see the German auto industry at is finest moment. It is of interest to know that shortly after their visit to the exhibit the entire auto industry was put to the task of supplying the necessary instruments of war that was set on capturing all of Europe. Again it was evident to all of them that this show was another of the opportunities to show the world about the New Germany as The Third Reich. After a while most in the group were somewhat fascinated by what they saw and what the New Germany was all about and were quite impressed.

All of the big name auto manufactures were there and included Ford, Mercedes, Opel, Audi, Horch, Skoda, BMW, Steyr, Tatra, DKW, Triumph, Victoria, Puch., Zundapp, etc. In addition companies who made component parts like Continental, Phillips, Notek, Helia, Jurid and Blaupunky were in attendance to show off their works. There were available, for purchase, soft cover books like Amtlicher Fuhrer which contained many pages of beautifully illustrated full color and black and white advertisements of the exhibitors at the show. In the first few pages of the book it explained the state of the world auto industry with great emphasis on the strength of the German auto industry-just another of the propaganda that they were being force fed about the Third Reich.

The bus ride through Berlin was most exciting as they saw the

German people in a very celebratory posture much different than what the folks back home knew about them mainly as a result of their losing WWI. It was almost as if Germany had risen form the ashes, like the Phoenix bird, and it was being advertised as the work of Adolph Hitler and The Third Reich.

CHAPTER EIGHT

After their visit to the Auto Show it was time for lunch so Hans took them to what the Germans call a Beer Cellar where they could sample outstanding German cuisine and many different beers mainly brewed in Germany. As before the Germans were very adept at putting their best foot forward so all would be impressed at all that was to be seen in Berlin. No doubt all of the people on the tour enjoyed the luncheon and then Hans prepared them for the next stops in the afternoon. After lunch, which they all enjoyed, the bus set out for the next stop. Along the way Hans pointed out the home of the Reich Security Minister, Heinrick Himmler. It was the home of the SS and the Gestapo. The building was stylish and certainly more inviting than the home of the Luftwaffe.

The next stop was to be at the Adolph Hitler's Reich Chancellery. This magnificent building that they saw driving up to the front was the work of Albert Speer and this was the seat of government of Adolph Hitler. They were escorted into the Chancellery for the tour. They were led up a grand stairway with plush carpeting to a vaulted entry hall. Easy to be seen were the bronze busts of Hitler and other leaders of the Third Reich. Some of the group had expressed the hope that they would get to see Hitler at work in his office but that did not happen. They did see a glimpse of his office but it was not occupied. No question this seat of The Third Reich was on a massive scale and there was no cost cutting on its erection. After a bit of time Hans asked them to follow him back to the bus so they could get to their next destination.

Their next visit would be to the Reichstag which was the building where the German legislature met. In January of 1939 Adolph Hitler made a rather detailed speech about the future of Germany. There were many articles at home appearing in the newspapers raising major concerns about the impact of the speech.

The following are excerpts from that speech:

"The National Socialist Movement has wrought this miracle. If Almighty God granted success to this work, then the Party was His instrument. We are indeed perhaps better able than other generations to realize the full meaning of those pious words "What a change by the grace of God".

Amongst the accusations which are directed against Germany in the so called democracies is the charge that the National Socialist State is hostile to religion. In answer to that charge I should like to make before the German people the following solemn declaration: 1. No one in Germany has in the past been persecuted because of his religious views (Einstellung), nor will anyone in the future be so persecuted... The Churches are the greatest landed proprietors after the State... Further, the Church in the National Socialist State is in many ways favoured in regard to taxation, and for gifts, legacies, & etc., it enjoys immunity from taxation.

It is therefore, to put mildly—effrontery when especially foreign politicians make bold to speak of hostility to religion in the Third Reich... I would allow myself only one question: what contributions during the same period have France, England, or the United States made through the State from the public funds? 3. The National Socialist State has not closed a church, nor has it prevented the holding of a religious service, nor has it ever exercised any influence upon the form of a religious service. It has not exercised any pressure upon the doctrine nor on the profession of faith of any of the Confessions. In the National Socialist State anyone is free to seek his blessedness after his own fashion... There are ten thousand and ten thousand of priests of all the Christian Confessions who perform their ecclesiastical duties just as well as or probably better than the political agitators without ever coming into conflict with the laws of the State... This State has only once intervened in the internal regulation of the Churches, that is when I myself in 1933 endeavored to unite the weak and divided Protestant Churches of the different States into one great and powerful Evangelical Church of the Reich. That attempt failed through the opposition of the bishops of some States; it was therefore abandoned. For it is in the last resort not our task to defend or even to strengthen the Evangelical Church through violence against its own representatives... But on one point it is well that there should be no uncertainty: the German priest as servant of God we shall protect, the priest as political enemy of the German State we shall destroy. I have not come into this world to make men better but to make use of their weakness.

In my life I have very often been a prophet, and have usually been ridiculed for it. During the time of my struggle for power it was in the first instance only the Jewish race that received my prophecies with laughter when I said that I would one day take over the leadership of the State, and with it that of the whole nation, and that I would then among other things settle the Jewish problem. Their laughter was uproarious, but I think that for some time now they have been laughing on the other side of their face. Today I will once more be a prophet: if the international Jewish financiers in and outside Europe should succeed in plunging the nations once more into a world war, then the result will not be the Bolshevizing of the earth, and thus the victory of Jewry, but the annihilation of the Jewish race in Europe!

"Speech to the Reichstag", 30 January 1939. Interestingly in April of 1939, Adolph Hitler made another provocative speech to the Legislature at the Reichstag which was in response to comments from President Roosevelt and served to be a major question of concern around the world. Following is an excerpt from that speech: "I have brought back to the Reich the provinces stolen from us in 1919; 1 have led back to their native country millions of Germans who were torn away from us and were in abject misery; I have reunited the territories that have been German throughout a thousand years of history-and, Mr. Roosevelt, I have endeavored to attain all this without bloodshed and without bringing to my people and so to others, the misery of war.

This I have done, Mr. Roosevelt, though 21 years ago, I was an unknown worker and soldier of my people, by my own energy and can therefore claim a place in history among those men who have done the utmost that can be fairly and justly demanded from a single individual.

You, Mr. Roosevelt, have an immeasurably easier task in comparison. You became President of the United States in 1933 when I became Chancellor of the Reich. Thus, from the very outset, you became head of one of the largest and wealthiest states in the world.

It is your good fortune to have to sustain scarcely 15 people per square kilometer in your country. At your disposal are the most abundant natural resources in the world. Your country is so vast and your fields so fertile, that you can insure for each individual American at least ten times more of the good things of life than is possible in Germany. Nature at least has given you the opportunity to do this.

Although the population of your country is scarcely one-third larger than that of Greater Germany, you have more than fifteen times as much room. And so you have time and leisure – on the same huge scale as you have everything else – to devote your attention to universal problems. Consequently the world is undoubtedly so small for you that you perhaps believe that your intervention can be valuable and effective everywhere. In this way, therefore, your concern and your suggestions cover a much larger and wider field than mine.

For my world, Mr. President, is the one to which Providence has assigned me and for which it is my duty to work. Its area is much smaller. It comprises my people alone. But I believe I can thus best serve that which is in the hearts of all of us – justice, well-being, progress and peace for the whole community of mankind.

Adolf Hitler

Their visit to the Reichstag was unimpressive and was merely another office building that one might see in the capital city of other major countries. After leaving the Reichstag they went through a part of Berlin that at first glance appeared to be a neighborhood where a large Jewish population lived as the signs on the store fronts led them to believe that. There were many signs with the Star of David on them. Several of the passengers, who no doubt were Jewish, commented on what they perceived to be Jewish Synagogues that were in rubble or in poor condition. Hans answer was that The

German government was in the process of rebuilding these Synagogues in other areas and they would be much improved and more modern. None of the group seemed to doubt Hans's answer except for the Jewish passengers who had heard rumors about the way the Jews were being treated in Germany. Not only did they see the ruins of Jewish Synagogues but the streets were bare of people and you could see people peeking out behind curtains in the residential areas. No doubt this scene had a major effect on all on the group.

It was late in the afternoon when the bus took them back to the hotel. Hans, over the loud speaker in the bus, told them to go to their rooms to rest and to be ready for the evening meal at a fine restaurant at the hotel. Both Chris and Pat were very moved by the sights they saw during the day. Back at their room in the hotel, they talked about the days adventures and they shared a major concern for the Jewish population in Germany.

At dinner they were served a meal of authentic German cuisine and flavored. Some of the same cheeses they were served at breakfast were available for dessert along with an array of fresh fruit and, of course, some special German pastries. Having eaten their full Pat and Chris made an early exit and retired to their room and to sleep as they would be traveling to another stop in Germany as the trip brochure indicated. Everyone seemed tired as it was a long and interesting day. Pat and Chris were happy to turn in early.

CHAPTER NINE

The loud noises coming from outside the hotel woke both Pat and Chris up. They looked at the clock and it was 6:30 in the morning, just barely getting light. When they opened the window overlooking the streets they saw people shouting and cheering and generally making an awful racket. Many of them looked like they had drunk too much beer as they were unsteady on their feet. Pat and Chris looked at each other and said "Wonder what that is all about?" Chris got dressed to go down to the lobby to find out what the devil was going on. It took him a few minutes to dress and since they were on the 2nd floor he walked down to the lobby. The scene, upon arrival in the lobby, was a sight to behold. In looking over the very crowded lobby he noticed some of the tour groups were already there. He approached a gentleman who he knew was from France and who spoke English. He seemed to be in control of his faculties while others seemed be in a state of shock and so Chris approached him and asked if he knew what was happening. Almost in a stutter, trying to get the words out, he said "The German military has invaded Poland and is in the process of over running the country with very little resistance. It appears to some that this is the beginning of the Third Reich government's try to take over the European Continent. This is a major problem for all on this tour for various reasons." They talked back and forth while some other members of the group joined the discussion. The Jewish members of the travel group seemed the most concerned about their welfare based on stories about the persecution of Jews in Germany and what they had seen during the day and the affect that would have on those in the group and for the rest of Jews in Germany. Of course the other folks were equally concerned regarding the potential escalation of the apparent war that had just begun. Chris, after listening to the comments of the others and listening to the cheers outside the hotel, became concerned about Pat and he being US citizens and how that might create a problem for them. Chris knew that both England and

France had signed a treaty with Poland that if Poland was attacked by the Germans that both England and France would come to their aide and declare war on Germany. After several more minutes of discussion and continued panic in the lobby, Chris tried to find their tour leader Hans. To his dismay he was nowhere to be found which created additional fear in all of them. They had come to rely on Hans, as the leader of the tour group, to help them out of potentially troublesome circumstances during the early days of this trip. Since they knew nobody else who could direct them in this potentially dangerous situation, the red flag was raised basically by the whole group. Chris decided to go back to his room and share with Pat the news, and to huddle with her in regard to what they needed to do.

In order to continue this story I think it would be helpful to talk about the events that began on the evening of August 31st 1939 and the beginning of WWII in Europe which found them front and center in Berlin.

The first month of the war that began in Poland had its genesis beginning on the 15th of June 1939. The Germans finalized their plans to attack Poland under the name "Plan White" which called for the destruction of the Polish Army before it could fully mobilize. On September 1, 1939 the first bombing of the war took place with targets being vital rail bridges and the Germans were successful in destroying them. Within hours the Polish campaign erupted into full scale war. The ground war invasion in the early hours of September 1, with 52 German divisions containing 1.8 million soldiers, pushed into Poland on 3 fronts. The use of Panzar tanks provided the Germans with the fire power on the ground plus the complimentary air strikes.

These tactics were used by the Germans during the first 2 years of the war as they were deemed very effective in crushing Poland. The Polish Government fled September 2 and the High Command followed 3 days later to Romania. On October 1, it was clear that continued resistance was pointless and Poland surrendered to Germany. Almost immediately the infamous SS began gathering Jews to be sent to the concentration camps or simply executed them on the spot. Thus, was the beginning of WWII in Europe.

CHAPTER TEN

After sharing with Pat what he had learned, Chris could see that she was at least as worried as he was. Their initial concern revolved around Hans. Since he was the tour guide he was very familiar with everyone on the trip. He knew their names. He knew their countries of origin. He knew they were at the hotel. He probably knew that most of them didn't know another soul in Berlin. Chris made the supposition that if Hans could be of value to them in getting out of Berlin and out of Germany and back home, he would not have disappeared. They were certain that based on his demeanor and the propaganda he was filling their minds with, he was loyal to Germany and the new Germany-The Third Reich under Adolph Hitler. Since everyone on the trip was European, except Pat and Chris, they were more concerned with their well being. All had come to Germany with their passports but Hans had taken control of them to keep them locked up and safe from theft. So here they were all of them without passports and without any contacts in Berlin.

Chris's first thought, regarding their safety, was to get in touch with the American Embassy to come and get them. They were most certain that the US had not entered the war so the embassy would be a safe haven for them. He picked up the phone dialing the front desk. He asked to be connected with the American Embassy and was told that all lines were down in the city and they could not connect me. He asked how long did they believe that the lines would be down. The answer he received was not comforting. They said "We have no idea". Although at this point they were not in a panic mode but they became more fearful of their safety.

He decided to go back down to the lobby and try and talk again with other members of the group with the hope that someone had a grand plan for safely leaving Germany. As Chris made his way to the lobby he spotted Hans on his way out of the Hotel with several Jewish members of the group along with several men in military uniforms. He was concerned at seeing this but was not sure what was going on. However, it did not look good. When Chris arrived at the desk a handful of the group were there. He was told the others had either gone back to their rooms or had just disappeared. Chris was dismayed with that news but sat down with the others and they were able to sit and explore their options. Jews in the group were not present so there was major concern for their welfare as he shared with the group about his seeing Hans leaving the Hotel with some of the Jewish couples along with what one would call military types. This was of major concern as they were certain that if they tried to leave the Hotel they would be stopped and asked for their papers which, of course, they did not have. So the option of leaving the hotel and seeking shelter and safety at their respective embassies did not seem to be an option. It would be too dangerous to leave the hotel and try to get their respective embassies as no one knew where they were. Among those in the lobby was Juan Carlos, the single gentleman from Spain who was seated next to Pat on the bus this morning and the young couple from Greece. All spoke English and we were able to speak to each other without having to have someone to translate. As they talked amongst themselves it was obvious to Chris that Juan Carlos was the most calm of all so he listened intently to what he was saying…

Juan Carlos discussed a number of ideas but not one of his ideas made sense. Chris asked everyone to go back to their rooms and discuss their situation with their traveling partners. Since he had a good feeling about Juan Carlos, Chris asked him to accompany him to his room where Pat and he could discuss the situation in the quiet.

Once they were settled in the room Chris called room service and ordered a large pot of coffee and some Danish pastries. By this time it was almost 9 in the morning and they were quite hungry not having had breakfast. In addition they needed the food to keep their energy up and also because they had no idea when they might be able to eat again. Pat and Chris visited with Juan Carlos while waiting for their food to arrive. It was important for the three of them to maintain a sense of urgency about their situation and not to let on to the waiter, who would bring them the food, the anxiety that the three had. Their breakfast, such as it was, arrived in about 40 minutes delivered by room service. They tried to portray a calm attitude but you could feel the tension in the air as they ate almost in silence.

After several minutes of discussion where all 3 of them expressed their concerns and possibilities, it became clear that the first order of business was to find someone in the hotel that might help them reach safety. Chris reached into a drawer on the table which had the phone on it and pulled out some stationary and a pencil so that they could take notes during this discussion. The list started to grow a bit as they listed everyone employed at the hotel that at least one of them had some contact with. They also attempted to list members of their group who might fit the profile of someone who could help them. Unfortunately they were unable to identify at least one individual in the group that they could seek help from.

They began the task of putting next to each employee of the hotel on the list what there was about them that might give them some reason to believe that they could help them. The individuals ran the gamut of chamber maids, wait staff from the restaurants, bar tenders, shop keepers and so on. The more they talked the more frustrated they became especially Pat who was definitely almost in tears. During this discussion Juan Carlos , who no doubt knew the Germans and Germany better than they did, shared a number of possible plans to get them out of Berlin and out of Germany. They had to find a way of getting out of the hotel without being stopped by those in the streets who had some authority to question them.. They came up with a rather ingenious plan.

Whoever they could get to help them that person needed to supply each of them with some sort of disguise that would not alert the police or the military. The plan was for each of them to dress in a costume that resembled a worker in the hotel. Maybe a chamber maid's attire for Pat. A doorman's attire for Chris and a handyman's outfit for Juan Carlos along with a tool box with hammer and other implements creeping out of the toolbox. So they agreed on this plan to get them out of the hotel. This meant that they would have to leave all of their clothing and other things back at the hotel except for the German Marks that they had exchanged for at the airport upon arrival in Berlin and their jewelry. The next order of business was to come up with a plan to get to a safe place where they could plan possible plan their options to exit Berlin and Germany.

In addition to the Marks they had, there were some rather expensive items of jewelry that they possessed including Pat's rather garish wedding and engagement rings. It was the general feeling that they might be able to bribe someone to help them out of the hotel and help them find a way out of Berlin. They made a list of their assets. They had about 1000 Marks plus a diamond drop and a diamond engagement ring. Juan Carlos recalled that he thought one of the chamber maids was also Spanish so they decided to let him try and find her and make a deal with her. They needed to keep at least 2/3rds of the Marks but they were willing to let go of the jewelry. With that information Juan Carlos left to find the Chamber Maid.

After about an hour Juan returned and talked about his meeting with the maid. " It took me a while to find her and she seemed somewhat taken back by my approach. I tried, the best I could, to explain our plan and asked her if she could help us. The plan that I shared with her involved the three costumes that we needed, the need for her to accompany us out of the hotel and to help us make our way to a safe house, she said that she would think about this and get back to us. I asked her to come to this room within the hour and let us know if she would help us and what we would need to give her to facilitate our escape from the hotel and from Berlin."

CHAPTER ELEVEN

After about 45 minutes there was a knock on their door and they opened it to find the maid. They ushered her in and began the conversation about her being willing to help them. Her reply was most encouraging but her demands were somewhat more than they had been willing to pay. She said with Juan Carlos translating" I will get the costumes for you which include a chamber maid costume for the woman, a doorman's attire for the Spanish gentleman and a handyman's attire for the other gentleman including a tool box. I will accompany all of you out of the hotel and bring you to my home where we will meet with my husband and my brother to try and help you out of Berlin. I will do all of this if you will give me all of the jewelry and the 500 Marks." Although the price was high they decided to do it as they really did not have an alternate plan as time was working against them. There was a lingering sense that perhaps the maid would turn them in after getting the price she asked for. They asked her to be back at the beginning of dark with the costumes as they thought they would have a better chance in the evening. They also thought that that time of day would be the time when the staff, who they represented, would be leaving work for the day. You could cut the air with a knife as the overriding feeling of anxiety permeated the hotel room as the maid left the room.

As the day wore on they could still hear the celebrations that were occurring outside the hotel. Peeking out the window they saw pretty much the same scene that they saw in the early morning. They ordered room service for lunch as they knew the maid would not be back until just before dark. They needed to keep most of the Marks they had so they decided to charge the lunch to their room. When the knock on the door came and was accompanied by "Zimmer service" they asked Juan to go into the bedroom and hide as they did not want to alert the room service person that there were 3 people in the room which was leased for just two. Chris signed the bill putting his room number down. The waiter did not seem to notice anything out of the ordinary so he said "Danke" and left. The lunch was a combination of different kinds of sausages, cheeses and German potato salad. They savored their lunch as they had no idea when they would have the opportunity to eat again. They were all on edge as the afternoon went by and were all wondering if the maid would show up. Pat continued to express her concern that after they gave the money and the jewelry to the maid she might not do her part of the bargain. Juan Carlos tried to reassure her and Chris that all would proceed according to their plan and, at this point, they had no choice but to trust her.

At about 5:30 the maid knocked on the door and entered as she had her master key that she used in cleaning the rooms. She pushed into the room with her usual cart of linens and towels, etc. She began to remove all the sheets and towels, etc. and exposed what appeared to be the three costumes that were part of the escape plan. They sorted them out and began to change their regular clothing with the new costumes. As they were doing this, the maid in Spanish, asked Juan for the money and the jewelry. The exchange having been made and the costumes changed into they were ready to make their way down the stairs and to leave the hotel. They were all very nervous but realized that they needed to be calm as not to raise attention to them. No need to talk to each other but a smile and a nod to those in this small group would work better than talking. Juan Carlos, in Spanish, asked the maid, that if there was any talking to be done with someone in the lobby or outside the hotel, to please respond for the group. The maid opened the door, peeked outside into the hallway, and motioned for all to follow her.

As they approached the lobby there continued to be bedlam and chaos which helped them as no one would pay attention to them on their journey to leave the hotel. They all tried to assume a non descript expression on their face so that they would be overlooked by everyone in the lobby. The plan was working as the occupants in the lobby were focused on their own set of problems. It worked so well that those few trip members who were in the lobby did not pay them any attention as they all were involved in conversation which Chris assumed had to do with the same concerns that they had.

As they stepped out of the hotel, it was quite amazing to see what was going on in the streets. People were cheering, singing patriotic songs and dancing and just having a glorious time. Other than pats on the back and directed smiles they were apparently not noticed by anyone, The thought came to Chris that they really did not have to dress in costumes not to be noticed but that was a chance they could not have taken. However, the costumes might be of assistance as the day wore on.

By this time it was almost dark and the street lights were coming on. A light rain began to fall which in a way served to obscure the group of four as they made their way into the darkness. Chris embraced the semi darkness and nodded his approval to the group. So far their plan was working but the feeling of apprehension was still in the air. Before they left their room in the hotel Juan Carlos informed them that the maid would be taking all of them to her home which was walking distance from the hotel. She also said that she lived with her husband and younger brother who were all from Spain and only her brother spoke some English but they all spoke some German. Her husband was a truck driver for a food distribution company that delivered all kinds of food in Berlin proper. Her brother was a delivery person for a large florist that had several locations in Berlin. It was her thought that her husband and her brother would be of great help to get them out of Berlin and Germany.

This was the time of year when the weather started becoming a bit cooler with the approach of Fall. The outside air was most refreshing and even the rain seemed to be a good sign. As they walked along they continued to see the revelry all around them with singing and dancing in the streets. This was good for them as no one was paying any attention. After a short walk, of about 5 blocks, they were led to a building that was two stories tall. There were two entrances which meant that there were two families living in this building; one family upstairs and one family downstairs. At home they would probably call this a duplex. The maid opened the door to the first floor apartment and, as she walked in, she turned on lights to the entry way. It appeared that the rest of the house was in darkness and that neither her husband or brother were at home. Juan Carlos had a brief conversation with the maid and then explained to them what she had said. It seems that both her husband and brother were still at work and would be home at about 7. In the meantime she was going to the kitchen to prepare a meal and she motioned for them to go into what appeared to be the living room. She told Juan Carlos that they should just relax and be thrilled that they had gotten this far.

Juan accompanied her into the kitchen and after a few moments he brought out a some bottles of beer and bottled water plus some crackers and some cheese that looked like Gouda from The Netherlands. Each of them were overly stressed and were just happy to sit and relax and reflect on this day that was coming to an end. There were many sighs coming from each of them as the period of relaxation was upon them. They did not seem to be overly hungry but they really appreciated the beer and water. Still they made quick work of the cheese and that contributed to their feeling of being somewhat secure and not in any immediate danger. It appeared that they were safe in that home at least overnight. Peeking out the window Chris saw that it was still sprinkling but he knew that the window shades and curtains needed to be closed so that no one would know they were there.

No question that the minutes that they were spending, prior to the arrival of husband and brother, gave them renewed energy. They were feeling somewhat more secure until Juan Carlos brought up a major concern that shook them all. He said that no doubt sometime later on in the evening or at the latest early tomorrow morning, Hans, our guide who was no doubt a Nazi sympathizer, would alert the authorities to our disappearance and there would be a notice sent out to the police and the military to be on the lookout for us. They would be given our descriptions which would make it easier for them to locate us. They had our pictures from our passports. Smiles turned to frowns and they all sensed the potential danger that lay ahead of them. True there was no doubt that they were in a safe place for the evening but when tomorrow came they had to be on their way trying to get out of Berlin and Germany. Juan talked further about his conversation with the maid. She told him at some point during the day she was able to contact her husband and brother and provide them with the entire information about this escape including what we were rewarding her for their combined help. She also went on to say that they were not in any way on the side of the Nazis as they recalled the civil war that occurred in Spain with rise to power of General Franco and his fascist government. The Civil War began in early 1936 and had basically ended in April of 1939. She saw many of her friends and relatives perish in the war. She was most fortunate to have left Spain with her husband and brother to emigrate to Germany shortly after the beginning of the Civil War.

While they were waiting for the husband and the brother, they talked about choices that they might explore about getting out of Berlin. Why were they afraid that the German's would try and stop them from leaving Germany? The first thing that came to mind was that Hans would tell the authorities that they had seen the destruction of the synagogues and the obvious mistreatment of Jews in Berlin. The picture they would paint would not be well received either in Europe, The United States, and elsewhere. In addition they would report the enthusiasm that the Germans had displayed about the aggressive invasion of Poland as shown by the revelry in the streets of Berlin.

Under the circumstances they needed to become invisible until they could work out a plan to exit Germany. Chris thought a bit and came up again with the idea of trying to contact the US Embassy in Berlin. Juan Carlos found the telephone directory, looked up the phone number for the US Embassy and dialed the number which was busy. He tried several times but always a busy signal. While they were still at the Hotel, Chris had tried to call the Embassy but was unable to make an outside phone call. It became obvious to them that somehow the Germans were not allowing any calls to be made to any embassies within the country. This was made clear as Juan Carlos tried to reach the Spanish Embassy and got the same busy signal. With the authorities everywhere there seemed to be no chance of their making it by foot to their respective embassies." Let's wait until the entire family is together and see what they might come up with", Chris said to the others and they were in agreement.

At a few minutes after seven they heard the front door open and the husband and brother came into the house. At the same time the maid came from the kitchen, greeted them and kissed them both on the cheek. Juan Carlos relayed what she said "This is my husband Ignacio and my brother Fernando" and then pointing at the three of them she said in Spanish" Let me introduce you to my friends from the United States Pat and Chris Casey and to Juan Carlos from Madrid". Handshakes and hugs all around as they greeted each other. Spanish people are very friendly and show that in their mannerisms when greeting those they do not know. After a brief pause, Ignacio and Fernando excused themselves to wash up and to change their clothing said Juan Carlos, who interpreted for them. Shortly there after they all sat down to enjoy a nice diner fixed by the maid. Chris said looking directly at the maid with Juan Carlos translating" You know you have never given us your name". After answering Juan Carlos told them "Her name is Senora Carolina Hortencia Ballesteros Obrigado." Wow what a long name, thought Chris and Pat, as they did not understand that Spaniards take the maiden name of their mothers and include it as part of their full name

They helped clear the table, wash and dry the dishes and then they all gathered in the living room. As a precaution Senora Carolina made sure all the curtains were drawn on the windows so that no one could see inside the house.

CHAPTER TWELVE

As they gathered in the living room the Senora excused herself and headed for the kitchen. In a few minutes she returned with several coffee cups, a tray of some kind of dessert that looked like custard and a pot of coffee. Juan Carlos said" This dessert is a specialty in Spain and is called Flan. It is a type of custard dessert and is very sweet and delicious. I know you will both enjoy it." By this time they were dead tired but the coffee and the sweets gave them new energy. Pat and Chris were especially inquisitive about what the Obrigado family might develop as a plan to help them. Ignacio was the first to talk, which was translated to them by Juan Carlos. There are three of you and no doubt the authorities have a description and they know that the husband and wife from America were traveling together. They also know that Juan Carlos was traveling alone. Therefore, in order to evade those who are looking for you, we feel it will be necessary for Juan Carlos and Mrs. Casey to leave together and for Mr. Casey we will need to find an alternate route out of the country."

You could see the wonder in Chris's eyes after he fully understood about the initial part of the plan which had he and Pat separated and she traveling with Juan Carlos. What did they know about Juan Carlos? Really not very much except that he was unmarried and came from Spain. Chris had a major problem in getting his arms around this plan so he asked Pat what she thought. She said" I don't want to go without you but Senor Ignacio makes a very good point about when they see me and Juan Carlos together they will not connect us and we would have a better chance of not being caught. In addition, you traveling by yourself in a different path that we take will be helpful also in aiding your escape. We need to consider that if only one of us gets back to the US while the other is detained in Germany at least our children will have one of us there for them."

Now it was time for Juan Carlos to give his opinion. He said "I do like this plan as it provides us with the best chance to get out of Germany. I personally believe that as you said, Pat, if only one of you gets out of Germany and back to the US, it will be a victory for your family back home. Also I believe that we should develop separate plans and routes to take to get out of Germany. It is better that we do not know the route that the other is taking as if caught it is probably a simple task for the Germans to get one to talk and disclose the others plan. They have ways to make you talk whether you want to or not." Still, it was apparent that Chris was not happy with the plan which required separation.

Fernando spoke up and said in English "I too believe that the plan my father has proposed will provide the best chance for at least one of you to escape from Germany. So if you agree, my family and Sr. Juan will discuss the plans this evening that we will share them with you in the morning. It is getting late so Carolina will show you to your bedroom and we hope that you will have a pleasant sleep. My father and I generally leave for work at about 8:15 so we will awaken you at 6Am and we will continue this conversation." So they said their good nights and Pat and Chris followed the Senora to their room. Pat and Chris were dead tired but they needed to take the time to discuss this plan regarding their separation with Pat going with Juan Carlos. There was no need to change their clothes as what they were wearing was all that they had. Pat said "I hope we can get several changes of clothes from the family".

It became very difficult for Pat and Chris to discuss this plan because neither of them wanted to be separated. What it came down to was the plan Ignacio shared with them was the best chance of at least one of them getting out of Germany. So they decided to sleep and talk about this tomorrow when they were more alert and not so tired; when they could think more clearly.

CHAPTER THIRTEEN

Chris had a big problem in falling asleep. He tossed and turned for a good deal of the night. He was having a hard time buying into the plan that Ignacio had come up with. Chris supposed that the idea of Pat and he splitting up, he alone and Pat with Juan Carlos, gave him pause to be concerned. After this restless sleep, even though the shades were drawn, he awoke with lots of light streaming into the room. For some reason he had concerns about Pat being with Juan Carlos for what would probably be an extended period of time. He tried to think what that was all about but he could not wrap his arms around any particular reason for that concern. Maybe it was just because they did not know much about Juan Carlos even though he has helped to get them to this safe house.

Chris looked over at Pat and she was still asleep. He did not want to wake her as she would need all the strength she could muster in the days to come. He wondered what the plans would be for their escape from Germany. He was not so much worried for himself as he had faced difficult times in his life and had been able to deal successfully with them. He believed his faith in the Lord would see them through but he remained somewhat anxious about what the three of them might face.

Chris dressed in the same clothes he had worn yesterday, used the bathroom and proceeded to find his way down to the kitchen. The clock on the wall read 6:40 and he saw Carolina making some coffee and toast with some help from Fernando. "Good morning he said. Can I help you do anything?: She replied with translation from Fernando" Buenos Dias. I am almost finished with the coffee and the bread but you can help me put the plates and cups on the dining room table. In the fridge you will find a few kinds of preserves, a carton of milk and some cheese and cold meats on a dish which you could set on the table. My husband will join us in about 15 minutes. We did not get to sleep until very late as we discussed the plans for you for today. Did you and your wife sleep well? Chris did not want to share his anxiety with her so he just said" We slept fairly well and, after I help set the table, I will go upstairs and make sure that my wife was preparing to come down."

As he went up the stairs the anxious feeling that he had upon awakening, took over his thoughts but again he could not find a reason for this except that the days ahead would be filled with much anxiety as they would hopefully find a way out of Germany. Pat was awake and taking a shower in the bathroom attached to the room they had slept in last night. Chris waited for her to finish toweling off and putting on her clothing. "Good morning darling. Did you have a good rest?" She ran over to Chris, put her arms around his neck and began to sob. Chris let her cry for a bit and he tried to be strong but she could sense that he too was worried. "Sorry for crying but I am scared big time about what happens from now on." she managed to say in between sobs.

Chris said "Yes, I too am concerned but I decided that for me the plan, which involved us splitting up, made some good sense as at the very least one of us could make it back home. We have to depend a great deal on Juan Carlos in getting you out of Germany. Although we do not know a lot about him he has been very helpful in getting us this far. As for me I believe whatever their plan is to get me home, I will be able to effectively execute the plan. Now that you are dressed, they are waiting for us downstairs with breakfast. We both need the nourishment so please eat a good breakfast".

When they met the others for breakfast downstairs, Carolina had cooked a large breakfast with eggs, sausage, toast and coffee. As they sat down to eat there was not much conversation as they all concentrated on enjoying the breakfast especially Pat, Juan Carlos and Chris. Since the plans had not been divulged, Chris thought this might be the last good meal that they would have in the days ahead. "Let's enjoy this breakfast before we talk about the plan" Fernando said, with a bit of uncertainty in his voice. Chris was most anxious to hear about the plans and nervously looked around the table at all the participants. There was an absence of smiles as he could see the seriousness of the moment.

As they were finishing their second cup of coffee, Fernando said "We first need to discuss the basis for the plan that we have come up with to see if you three agree. If you will remember our thinking was that the three of you should split up with Pat and Juan Carlos paired and with Chris on his own. I believe that the plans we have come up with have an excellent chance of success. Another part of the plan was for Chris not to know Pat's and Juan Carlos's plan and vice versa. Do each of you agree with these two parts of the plans?". Chris said "I believe I can speak for my wife and for myself to say that we agree on the plan so far but we do this with great reservations. The idea that basically won us over was that if only one of us got back to our family at home it was worth taking the risk of splitting up" He could see that there were tears streaming down Pat's face so he put his arms around her to try and comfort her. Juan Carlos, who had been very quiet this morning, also agreed to the plan as it now existed.

As Fernando began to speak Chris asked Carolina for another cup of coffee which she, smiling, poured for him. "As you three have agreed so far, it will be necessary for Chris to retire to the bedroom as we discuss the plan for Pat and Juan Carlos. Again we must insist that no one shares their plan with the others." Chris gave Pat a hug and retired upstairs to await their calling him back. As he walked up the stairs it was almost like his whole life was on screen before him. He remembered people saying that when one is in trouble and their life is in danger, this kind of thing took place. As he walked in the door of the bedroom, he closed the door as not to hear what was going on downstairs. For a brief moment he thought that he could safely sit on the stairs to overhear what was being said. He discarded that thought having thought better of it as it related to the overall planning process. So he lay down on the bed and prayed a bit for the safety of the three of them.

Fernando began to share their plan as soon as he felt that Chris was out of earshot from them. "Pat, you need to know something about Juan Carlos that he failed to share with you. Having lived in Spain all his life, he served as a player in the Civil War that has just ended. His family has been prominent in politics in Spain for a number of years. In fact, Juan Carlos is a first cousin to Generalissimo Franco who, as you probably now is the head of the new Government in Spain. The war that lasted over three years is now over but the future for Spain lies in how well Franco governs. Juan Carlos has an extensive resume of schooling which includes a PHD degree in Economics from the University of Berlin. So as you can see he not only is familiar with Berlin but he also has that relationship with General Franco in Madrid. The plan that the General had discussed with Juan Carlos was that after assuming power at the wars end, he would appoint Juan Carlos to be Minister of the rebuilding of Spain's economy. So, the bottom line is that the General is most anxious to have Juan Carlos back home. The authorities, here in Berlin, will not take even a second look at the two of you as you leave this house this morning because, as a couple, you do not resemble the couple they are looking for."

Fernando went on to say" On the way to work this morning my father and I will drive you to the Spanish Embassy and, when there, plans will be made to get both of you together out of Berlin and to Spain. So, Pat, as you can see, the plan is almost foolproof. New passports will be provided to both of you by the embassy as you travel as man and wife on your journey to Madrid. Since the relationship between Hitler and Franco is extremely positive I see no reason why this should not happen as I have explained it. Do you have a comment, Senor Juan Carlos?"

"Pat, as you and Chris retired last night I did not. I spent the next few hours letting this family, who are from Spain, know about my position in Spain and my relationship with General Franco. It was fairly obvious that the plan, which Fernando has explained, has a great chance of success. At the most it should only take a few days to get to Madrid where the rest of the plan will be exercised. As we are not able to contact the Spanish Embassy here in Berlin by phone, it does make the plan somewhat more difficult as it depends on the guards at the Embassy allowing us to enter. If the guards balk I will ask them to talk to their superiors as they will confirm my station. The reason why I was included in your tour group was that the General wanted me to vacation and specifically in Germany so that I could report back to him about my observations while in Germany. All in all this is a plan that will work to get both of us safely out of Germany."

Fernando followed "Since my father and I will leave for work in about 15 minutes, both of you need to be ready. Carolina is providing Pat with new attire and, since I and Juan Carlos are about the same size, I will provide a change of clothing for Juan Carlos. Pat, please follow Carolina to her bedroom where you can change clothes and Juan Carlos will accompany my father to my bedroom to do the same. You both must hurry so the timing is perfect to get to the embassy. After we are gone Carolina will call Chris to come downstairs. By that time we will be gone. I know that Pat, your not saying goodbye to Chris and he to you, will be difficult but necessary. We cannot afford to take a chance that one of you will force the other to share the plan. This must not happen so that is why you must be separated." Juan Carlos and Pat left the room to change their clothes. Pat was feeling both anxious and sad about her not saying goodbye to Chris but she understood the sequence of events in the plan. Uppermost was the need for at least one of them to get back home to the United States.

Hugs were the order of the day as Juan Carlos and Pat embraced Carolina and thanked her for her help. She led them out to the waiting car driven by Ignacio with Fernando trailing the group. As they drove away they waved out the back window at Carolina and were soon rounding the corner on the way to the Embassy. Juan Carlos tried to comfort Pat as the tears began to flow down her cheeks. "It is sad to leave your husband but he will be ok. In the meantime we need to focus on the plan to get us out of Berlin."

Carolina, once back in the house, called upstairs in Spanish for Chris to come back down. Chris understood and came down the stairs and was clearly dumbfounded to find only Carolina in the breakfast room. In a somewhat angry voice he said "Where the hell is everyone? Where is my wife? What the hell is going on?" Carolina did not fully understand but she could tell that he was angry. She said in Spanish "Please calm yourself. I will call Fernando at his work so that he can answer your questions" The only thing Chris understood was Fernando. So he assumed he would hear shortly from Fernando. After about 30 minutes he saw Carolina on the phone which she handed to him. Fernando said" You may recall that the plan was that neither you nor Pat knew the plan for the other. If you or Pat were apprehended the Germans would find a way to make you talk. So, as one of the most important parts of the plan for escape it was necessary for Pat and Juan Carlos to leave here prior to your coming down stairs. I can assure you that their plan has better than a 75% chance of success and that the plan for you is a bit more difficult and therefore has a lower chance of success. You will need to stay here, undetected, until I return from work this evening with my father and then we can talk some more."

Chris was in a state of shock. To think that he was not able to hug and kiss his wife, before she left, was devastating. He wondered what was going thru Pat's mind when she found out that saying goodbye to him was not going to happen. As he looked back at the last few days, it almost seemed like a bad dream and that he will no doubt wake up shortly. There was not much he could do as neither Carolina nor her family would tell him what the plan was for Pat. He needed to be in a good frame of mind when they divulge his plan this evening. So he decided to lie on the bed and try and relax. Sleep was impossible as thoughts were just racing through his mind. All kinds of scenarios popped up most of which were not positive. No doubt, he napped from time to time. He looked at the clock after a while and it showed 11:45AM so he probably did nap. He was hungry so he went down to the kitchen, opened the fridge and looked for some food to eat. There was a plastic bowl wrapped with some kind of plastic. Opening it he found a rather large piece of chicken. He also noticed some white wine and a few bottles of beer. No wine for him so he opened a bottle of beer and ate the chicken. Upon finishing he felt a bit better so he thought what next. He saw a radio which he turned on but all he could get was in German so he turned off the radio. He retired again to the bedroom upstairs. He began to think of the kids back home. They are probably worried having not heard from them especially with the war going on. Hopefully, either Pat or himself, once they are out of Germany, will get in touch with them and let them know what has gone on. He stayed in his room until about 5:30 when he heard the front door shut downstairs. Carolina yelled "Senor Chris"

He went into the bathroom, slapped some cold water on his face and climbed down the stairs. Hearing voices in the kitchen, he went there and Fernando and Carolina and Ignacio were talking in Spanish and he understood a word or two but that was it. Fernando smiled and addressed him saying "I am sorry that we had to be secretive about what the plan was for your wife and Juan Carlos. Since they felt this was best in order to give one of you the best chance to get out of Germany. Although I can't tell you the whole plan I can tell you that we delivered Juan Carlos and Pat to the gate at the Spanish Embassy. I saw them open the gate to let them in but we needed to leave immediately so I don't know what happened after we left. Chances are that they were welcomed into the Embassy and then the rest of the plan could proceed".

Hearing this Chris was overjoyed with the news. As Juan Carlos was a citizen of Spain the fact that they were allowed beyond the front gate was encouraging. "When will we know if their plan to get out of Germany was successful" Chris said. Fernando replied" It will be a couple of days and if they are successful, Juan Carlos will call us to give us the news. If the entire plan was not successful, he will share that news with us. My belief is that there is an excellent chance that the entire plan will be completed favorably. Since we must wait a few days, you need to stay here in this house until we hear from them. Then, we can discuss the plan to try and get you out of Berlin. That is the best we can do for now so relax, rest and enjoy Carolina's cooking and enjoy some good German white wine."

Carolina and Ignacio brought out some cheese, crackers and some white wine and brought them into the living area where they all sat down to enjoy the food and wine. Chris was feeling a bit of relief although he knew that there was still a very good chance that the plan for Pat and Juan Carlos might not have succeeded. He asked Fernando what news did he have about the war and the German invasion of Poland. He said" The German people are still celebrating the invasion and appear to remain positive about the road that Hitler had informed them of his earlier speeches about the New Germany and The Third Reich. I also have heard that the authorities have begun rounding up all the Jews in Poland and sending them by rail to concentration camps somewhere in the country. This in many ways goes back to some of the comments made by Adolph Hitler about developing a pure race of Germans and taking control of those people who don't fit the mold and or are potential saboteurs of the process. It also appears that all the German Jews are being rounded up, men, women and children and to be taken to similar concentration camps. I certainly would not want to be a Jew under the circumstances." Chris said "Would you ask your sister what was going on back at the hotel after she arrived for work this morning? Asking Carolina in Spanish, he translated what she said "There was still a great amount of confusion. It looked like the authorities were interrogating those who were part of your tour and were still in residence at the hotel. I looked for the leader of your group, the German named Hans, but he was nowhere to be found. I went about my work and sometime in the early afternoon the authorities wanted to question the entire working staff at the hotel. They questioned me and the only information I could give them when asked about Herr and Frau Casey was that when I entered their room to make up the beds and clean the room there was no one there. They asked me if there were clothing and other things that belonged to them and I said yes and they are probably still in the room. I was then excused.

Carolina excused herself to go and finish preparing dinner. After the cheese and the wine Chris was really not that hungry but decided that if he declined to eat dinner it would be rude. Carolina, with help from her husband, brought out some chicken, rice (They guessed it was Spanish rice) and some bread and butter. Listening to the conversations of the family Chris was beginning to pick up some Spanish words like pollo (chicken) pan(bread) agua (water) cerveza (beer) cocina (kitchen) bano (bathroom) trabajo (work) and so forth. Even knowing a few words did not lead to any conversations in Spanish. He just continued to ask Fernando to translate for him.

The mood seemed to be somewhat positive but, for Chris, the anxiety was in evidence. Were they putting on a positive face for his benefit? He did enjoy the dinner and he ate most of what he had put on his plate. He decided not to have any more alcohol that was offered to him as he wanted to be as alert as possible that night and over the next few days. Having no idea what the plan would be that would be revealed to him after they get word from Juan Carlos, the need for calming and attentiveness was paramount in his mind.

CHAPTER FOURTEEN

After dinner there was not much to say, and since only two of them spoke English, the conversations were limited. Chris asked Fernando if there was a way of getting word to our children back in the United States. "It appears that the Germans have made it almost impossible to make calls or send wires out of the country. There is a good chance that when Pat and Juan Carlos are safe she will make it a priority to get word to them about the situation here in Europe' Fernando went on to say "As I said earlier there should be word from Juan Carlos in the next 48 hours".

"They all retired early but before they went to their bedrooms Ignacio (translated by Fernando) said Senor Casey, please be patient over the next few days and try and be positive about the success of the plan for Pat and Juan Carlos. You will have to remain in our home with the shades drawn so that nobody can see into our home and see you. Feel free to eat whatever is available in our fridge and get some really good rest which will prepare you for the days ahead. Buenos noche, Chris."

Chris went to his room, undressed, took a shower in the family bathroom and crawled into bed. It was fairly early in the evening, quite a bit earlier than when he was used to going to sleep. This early time contributed to his not being able to fall asleep. He continued to think about all the possible scenarios, mostly bad, that could occur that would prevent their escape from Germany. As he lay there and thought of all the negatives a scenario, a really ridiculous one, entered his mind. He agreed to send Pat along with Juan Carlos, who they knew very little about, on a journey that would hopefully lead to an escape from Germany. His mind began to wander trying to recall, in his minds eye, the time or times that Pat and Juan Carlos were together with or without his presence. Did he miss something about their interaction? Now this was getting weird. How can one think that there was a possibility that a casual relationship had turned into something more?

Was he getting paranoid? They were only together for a brief period of time before they left the hotel to come here. Absurd! There is no reason for him to think these kinds of thoughts but he could not help himself. Guess all of the stress is finally wearing him down and allowed him to think such improbable thoughts. The more he had these thoughts the more the difficulty he had to fall asleep. He decided to go downstairs very quietly, look around a bit, listen to the sounds outside the house. As he moved slowly down the stairs, he overheard a conversation that was in progress with Carolina, Ignacio and Fernando. It was in Spanish so he had no idea of what they were saying so he turned around and went back to bed. He would ask them in the morning what that was all about. All of the tension made him somewhat sleepy so after a few minutes he was fast asleep.

When he awoke the next morning he looked at the wind up clock on the bedside table and it showed 6:44. As he lazily laid there he tried to recall if he had any dreams that he could remember from last night. Over the years he had found that one of the ways God interacts with him is through dreams. Nothing came to mind. Although he was a practicing Christian, his relationship with the Lord was just ok and left much to be desired. Never was much for solitary prayer but at this moment he felt he was being encouraged to pray and so he did. "Dear God. I know you are there and I am sorry that I have not had the best relationship with you. At Church, many times during the sermons from the Priests, I was reminded that you are always there for us and that you love us unconditionally. I come to you now hoping you will receive my prayer and be generous with your love for myself, Pat, and my family. I have been told, at Church, that you, in the form of the Holy Spirit, are always at our side. So, please watch over Pat and I as we try to make our way home. Also be with our kids back home and give them a sense of security as the next few days go on and bring us home safely." That really felt good. Why have I not, in prayer, spoke to the Lord either asking for forgiveness, thanking him for all the blessings in my life and for His protection of my family and my friends?

He got out of bed and went into the bathroom. He noticed that someone had left a toothbrush and toothpaste next to the sink. How thoughtful he thought. After brushing he` hand washed himself and dried himself and as he walked out of the bathroom, he saw his clothes on the chair next to the bed. He really needed a change of clothes as he thought a new look would be helpful for having a positive attitude. He did dress and went down the stairs. Everyone was in the kitchen drinking coffee and Carolina offered me a cup and he said "I really could use a cup of strong coffee this morning as I had a difficult time getting to sleep last night". Although Fernando did not translate his words to the others Chris had a feeling that they understood what he was saying. Carolina said something in Spanish which Fernando relayed to Chris:" I am sorry that I cannot make a big breakfast for you this morning as I have to leave early for work. After we all leave for work please help yourself to whatever is here in the kitchen," Chris said 'Gracias". At the very least he could say thank you in Spanish. Before they all left Fernando said" Please do not answer the phone if it rings as there is not be anyone at home here during the day".

As the day wore on he tried to think of things he could do to amuse himself. He looked everywhere hoping to find something to read, a book or a magazine, that was written in English but no luck. He did have a second cup of coffee with some left over pastry of some kind he tried to identify it but was unable. Looking in the pantry, which was quite small, he saw a box of Kellogg's Corn Flakes on one of the shelves. Finding a cereal type bowl in the kitchen cabinet, he poured some cereal into the bowl, added some sugar and found a bit of milk in the refrigerator. Wow. Corn Flakes in Berlin!

In the afternoon he thought he would try and take a nap to catch up on the sleep he had lost last night. He went up the stairs into his bedroom. It was the Fall of the year so he thought he would open a window to let some refreshing air into the room which might help him take a good nap. Good idea. It worked and he dozed off for maybe an hour or so. When he awoke he felt better, looking at the clock it said 4:50. Based on what he remembered her schedule to be, Carolina would be home in about an hour with Fernando and Ignacio returning shortly thereafter. He remembered that he wanted to ask them what they were talking about when he had heard them last night as he was coming down the stairs.

He spent the next hour trying to rid himself of the demons that keep entering his mind. So many negatives were moving his anxiety level to a new high. Perhaps this would be the night that they hear from Pat and Juan Carlos. At a bit after 6PM he heard the front door open and peeked down the stairs and saw Carolina moving towards the kitchen. Since he could not understand her and she could not understand him he decided to wait for Ignacio and Fernando to come home and then he would walk downstairs. He thought he heard Carolina call his name but he did not answer so she might think that he was napping. One good thing about being by himself the last 2 days was that he took occasional naps which helped to energize himself. "Lord knows what I will face over the coming days."

He could hear Carolina busying in the kitchen which hopefully meant they would have a regular meal that night for dinner. At a few minutes after 7PM the front door opened and he heard the family greeting each other so it was time for him to make an appearance. Whatever Carolina was cooking, it smelled wonderfully and, after a day of not much food, he was ready for dinner. Hugs all around as he entered the kitchen. As per usual Ignacio and Fernando were all about bringing wine and cheese into the living area. He figured out that this must be either a Spanish custom or a European custom but, whatever it was, he enjoyed it. In fact, he made a mental note that when Pat and he were united again back home they should copy this custom.

After a bit of time Carolina went back to the kitchen and then announced that supper was ready. Chris thought he recognized a few words like comida and ahora which he thought meant food and now. They all went into the dining room and Ignacio had brought the bottle of wine to the dinner table and filled the glasses that they brought from the living area. There was a massive bowl in the center of the table and not much else except for some pan (which he knew meant bread). The smell was really something so he asked Fernando what was in the big bowl. He said" It is called paella which is a typical Spanish dish. It has chicken, pork sausage, shrimp and yellow rice. We don't have it very often because it is quite expensive to buy the ingredients. This is a treat for all of us so get busy eating". Chris chuckled a bit about this attempt at some humor and he did what Fernando said taking the ladle and scooping out the paella. He was hungry and would have enjoyed almost anything Carolina cooked for dinner but the fact is he could not remember eating anything as delicious as this. Fernando watched him wolf down the food and he said" Don't hurry there is plenty for seconds". In some way he was beginning to consider himself one of the family as they did all they could to support him during this very hard time. He was grateful and would try to show his gratitude if only by words of thanks.

After dinner he decided to help clear and wash the dishes as a small token of thanks and he really enjoyed doing that. Chris asked Fernando when he thought they might hear from Pat and Juan Carlos." "I hope that it would be this evening as they would not call in the daytime since they would know we three would be at work. They would have no idea that you were still here with us as they had no idea about your plan for escape thinking that you were probably gone" Fernando explained.

No sooner, had they moved into the dining area again to enjoy some coffee, then the telephone rang. Chris jumped up to answer the phone but Fernando motioned for him not to do as he would. He was hopeful and excited to hear who was on the phone. "Bueno," he spoke on the phone, Como estas Juan Carlos Donde esta?" Chris was overjoyed to hear the name Juan Carlos. Fernando spoke in Spanish for the most part during the lengthy conversation. Fernando handed the phone to Chris and on the other end Pat spoke to him. She said that she was safe and that she hoped he was ok. She went on to say that Juan Carlos gave Fernando all the information about their journey and that he would share it with him. She also said that they would be joining us in a few days in Berlin and that all would work out. Chris replied "How is that possible that you and Juan Carlos would be coming back to Berlin. It makes no sense to me" barely getting the stuttering words out of his mouth. "Fernando will explain the whole thing to you. Please put Fernando back on the phone so that Juan Carlos can complete the details of what will happen next. I love you and miss you." Before handing the phone over to Fernando he said that he loved her too. He was a bit surprised to hear that they would be coming back to Berlin. He could not imagine under what conditions it would make sense for them to come back to Berlin when the plan was to escape Germany.

Fernando said his good byes on the phone and then saying to all "Please all sit down (in English and in Spanish). I will try to tell you the whole story about their escape from Berlin. It is truly remarkable that everything went as planned. They are safe and not to worry. You will recall I said that I was able to get them to the front of the Spanish Embassy, saw someone open the gates and let them in. At that point I had no idea what happened next. Juan Carlos explained that they were taken into the Embassy and directed to a rather small conference room. They were asked to be seated and to await the Spanish Ambassador or his assistant. After a short wait he said in came a gentleman in a well cut suit who introduced himself as Joachim Hernandez, the assistant to Colonel Enrico Juarez, the Spanish Ambassador to Germany. The good news for Pat was that Sr. Hernandez spoke in English. Pat wondered if every Embassy requires those in charge to be as well dressed as he was? His manner was quite cordial.

Senor Hernandez first asked for their passports and shared this story with him. Juan Carlos went on to say "I am Juan Carlos Fortunato, a Spanish citizen living in Madrid. I was in Berlin to begin a bus tour through Germany. On the first evening at the hotel in Berlin there was cocktail party which was attended by all the members of this tour group and the tour guide Hans; I did not get his last name. During the party I was introduced to a couple from the United States; Chris and Pat Casey."

"This lady I am with is Pat Casey. Her husband is in hiding in Berlin hoping that I might arrange in some way for his escape from Germany which, by the way, is the reason why we have come to the Embassy. The reason we don't have our passports is because, the tour leader Hans asked us all to give him our passports that as they would be safer in his possession. When we learned of the invasion of the Germans into Poland, which we assumed would be the start of a war, we all felt that we should try to get out of Germany before things became dangerous for the three of us. Since we had been exposed to many things on our first day touring including the decimation of the Jewish Synagogues, we thought that the Germans would not allow us to leave and to let the world know what was happening in Berlin including the obvious joy that Berliners expressed for the invasion.

"After learning about the invasion and listening to the shouting in the street outside the hotel, we developed a plan to get us out of the hotel and to a safe house. I explained the details of the plan for the three of us and we were helped by a Spanish family that lived in Berlin, the woman working as a chamber maid at the hotel we were at. We offered her money and jewelry and, after speaking with her husband, she agreed to help us. She provided us with disguises to get us out of the hotel where we would not be exposed as members of the tour group. This was further complicated because Hans, our group leader, was a confessed member of the Nazi party and would give our descriptions to the authorities."

"We made it out of the hotel and were directed by Carolina, the maid, to her residence nearby. She asked that we make ourselves comfortable awaiting the return of her husband and brother from work. It was a about an hour or so when her relatives came home. We were introduced to each and were told that Carolina had informed her husband and brother about our possible escape from Berlin."

After dinner Fernando, who was the only one in the family that spoke English, said that he wanted me, Juan Carlos, to remain in the living area to discuss the plans while Mr. and Mrs. Casey retired for the evening. And so after their going to bed, I began to share the following story to the family. As I have told you my name, Juan Carlos Fortunato, what you do not know is that I am a cousin of General Franco. I played a rather important part in the Civil War, and, as a reward the General appointed me to be a major player in his government. He also gifted me with a completely paid vacation in Germany. You see that earlier in my life I went to school at the University in Berlin to get my doctorate. So this is how we come to you today asking for your assistance in getting myself and Senora Casey to Madrid."

"That is quite a story Senor Fortunato, said Sr Hernandez. Just incredible. It will be necessary for me to call Madrid to verify who you are and, if all is well, ask for the assistance in getting you to

Madrid. So, since both of you are no doubt hungry, I will ask the kitchen to prepare a luncheon meal for you to be served in this room. If you will please excuse me, as I go about my business, I will be back to you as soon as I have the information I need."

"We made ourselves comfortable while waiting for the return of Senor Hernandez. Pat expressed her amazement on what I just told the Senor." How come you never told us who you really are and the influence you can bring to bear on our ability to escape Berlin. Did my husband know? Did the family know who you are?' I told the family that the first night we were there, and after you and your husband went to bed, the family and I discussed the plan for the three of us to escape. I knew that the Ballesteros family had emigrated to Germany prior to the Civil War in my country and also knew that they were on the opposite side of the fence in regard to my position and the position of the General. I was hopeful that they would overlook this and be cooperative in helping us to leave Berlin in safety."

"The plan that we made, which was in two separate parts, providing Pat and I a much better chance of escape than the plan for Chris. I also felt some sort of connection with Pat so that made it easy for me to go with the plan for Pat and I which the four of us decided on. You might call this connection one of infatuation but we have done nothing to be ashamed of at this point."

"The meal that was served to us was ok as we were both very hungry. It consisted of cheese, cold meats, bread and a half bottle of wine. Pat still seemed anxious about all that was happening and said "I am still in a state of shock and wonder why you did not share your position with my husband and myself?"

I tried to reassure her that it was necessary if the plan for the two of us would work. She was trying to fight back tears saying "What about Chris? Is his plan one that would safely get him out of Berlin and will you tell me now about his plan". I held her hand in a loving way and told her that she will be made aware of the plan for Chris once we get to Madrid."

"My attempt to comfort Pat was not working and I could feel the tension in the room. At this point, thank goodness, Senor

Hernandez re-entered the room with a broad smile on his face." "Senor and Senora I had told your story to a high ranking official in Madrid and, after a while, he called me back to say that Generalissimo Franco had confirmed who you are and will be calling you here in Berlin to explain the plan that he will put into motion immediately." "Needless to say, I was overjoyed with the news but Pat showed no emotion and I could see that she was still very anxious about the proceedings."

Coffee and pastries were served to us while we waited for the call from Madrid. I continued to try and make Pat more comfortable but with no success. She did not say a word but did drink some coffee and had a taste of a pastry. I felt that she was trying to keep her strength up without having any idea what would happen next. Shortly before evening Senor Hernandez brought a phone into the room and plugged it into an outlet on the wall. He handed me the phone and I said Bueno. Hearing very clearly the voice of my cousin, the General, he inquired about my health and was I being well taken care of at the Embassy. I reassured him that I was well and that the staff of the Embassy had been most cordial. He began to outline the plan for our leaving the Embassy and flying to Madrid where we would be safe."

"Here is his plan. Since we did not have our passports the staff at the Embassy would issue new passport for each of us indicating that we were husband and wife. Photos will be taken and attached to the passports to give us credibility. Because he and Adolph Hitler had a very good relationship, he called him and asked a favor. Would he grant safe passage to me and Pat who were traveling as man and wife? Hitler agreed and said he would send his personal driver tomorrow morning to escort us to the airport where there would be a plane to fly us to Madrid. The General went on to wish us safe voyage and looked forward to meeting us in Madrid at his residence. I thanked him and I also said that I looked forward to seeing him in Madrid. We said our goodbyes and I hung up the phone. Senor Hernandez said that he was fully aware of the General's plan and that he would make us comfortable awaiting the events to take place tomorrow morning."

"After the phone call from Madrid I was able to relax and had the sense that we would be ok and that we would be in Madrid in a relatively short time. Pat continued to be anxious and, again, I tried to assure her about the success of our plan but all she could say was that she feared for her husband's escaping from Berlin. She went on to say that she understood what would happen to her but she was more concerned with the fate of Chris. Without divulging my plan for Chris, I assured her that she need not worry about Chris for we will be joining him shortly. We need to relax, enjoy the hospitality of the Embassy for the rest of the day and then be prepared to leave Berlin tomorrow morning on our way to Madrid."

Fernando explained "That is the entire report from Juan Carlos. I am pleased that Juan Carlos and Pat have come as far as they have and that tomorrow they will have their escape to Spain and , Chris, the plan for your escape will get underway. Tomorrow, when my uncle and I return from work, we should have heard from Juan Carlos and that he and Pat are safe in Madrid and then I will share with you the plan for your escape. In the meantime we all need to retire with the sense that all will be well. So, Chris, I bid you good night and look forward to the morrow when we can talk about the plan for your escape."

CHAPTER FIFTEEN

On the morning of the next day Pat awakened after hearing a knock on her bedroom door. She was a bit confused as to where she was as the past few days had been so confusing and her anxiety level was high. She called out to see who was knocking and Juan Carlos replied: "Pat, it is time for you to get up as the car that Hitler is sending should be here before the hour is up. Look in your bathroom and you will find a change of clothing to wear on our plane trip to Madrid. I have in my possession the passports that the Embassy has provided for us to help get us out of Berlin. There is a modest breakfast available in the room where we spent most of yesterday. I will greet you there".

At the same time, in the home of the Ballesteros family, Chris arose from what turned out to be a fairly peaceful sleep. He heard some talking from the downstairs but could not make out what was being said because it was mostly in Spanish. He went into the bathroom to shower and noticed that someone had left out a strait razor with shaving cream soap in its ceramic container and a brush for the cream. The toothbrush and paste was still there from yesterday so he brushed my teeth and then showered. The warm water felt very soothing as the spray from the shower hit his body. Quite refreshing. He realized he had not shaved for several days but thought that maybe he should not shave as the stubble was somewhat of a disguise. The authorities certainly have his passport which Hans no doubt had given them. So the decision was not to shave. He had the sense that he would be faced with so many more important decisions if he were back home at work.

He dressed wearing the same clothes he had on yesterday. Since he spent the entire day in the house the clothes were neither soiled or smelly. He welcomed the new day with great anticipation as, based on what Fernando had said the night before, he would be on his way to escaping Germany. On one hand he was joyful at the prospect of leaving Germany but was also apprehensive about the part that Pat and Juan Carlos might play. If he heard Pat correctly she said that she and Juan Carlos would meet with him soon here in Berlin. He continued to have a difficult time in understanding how that could possibly be part of his escape plan. So he ventured into the new day and walked down the stairs. As usual the family were all together in the kitchen. The smell of strong coffee attracted him so he took a cup that was on the counter and filled it from the pot that was heating on the stove. He bid good morning to everyone saying it in Spanish: Buenos Dias Senor Ignacio, Senor Fernando and Senora Carolina. They all laughed at his attempt to speak to them in their native language.

Fernando was the first to speak" Senor Chris, today should be the beginning of the completion of the plans for you, Pat and Juan Carlos to all escape from Germany permanently and especially for you and Pat to begin your return home to your family. We will hear from Juan Carlos to tell us about their safe passage to Madrid and what would transpire from there. I have asked him to call me at home after 7PM this evening and at that time we will know more. So again, you will need to remain here with the shades drawn and to await our return home in anticipation of a call from Madrid. Please make yourself as comfortable as you have been able to and hope that the hours of this day pass quickly. Please feel free, again, to eat whatever is available in the refrigerator. On the way home last night I stopped at a book store and purchased a book of short stories from your well know author Edgar Allen Poe It is written in English. I hope it will help you pass the time. See you this evening." With that Carolina, Ignacio and Fernando bid their: "adios" to him and left the house.

Not used to spending this much time alone. Everyday it seemed like that. He missed Pat and the children. Why didn't he ask Pat if she got word to the kids? He was not thinking clearly. He had spent his entire career dealing with problems that require sound thinking. He guessed the stress here was too much for him to handle and to wrap his arms around. He thought back on times when he was conflicted and when he was ambivalent, or had a tough decision to make. What did he do? Simple! God is always in control of his life so simple prayer had always been comforting so he prayed" Lord God you have been at my side all the days of my life. I have continued to be thankful of all the blessings that you have provided to me. Please watch over my wife Pat and also Juan Carlos who is apparently being a tremendous support to her. Also keep our kids back home safe and give them the strength to get through while not hearing from us. Give me the strength to overcome all of my fears, to allow me to think straight and to make good decisions. Thank you for putting the Ballesteros family in our lives and keep them safe as they have been taking a big chance helping us. Bring Pat and I together and grant us the peace that we need and help us to get back home safely. Help me overcome the negative thoughts that I have had about Pat and Juan Carlos. I know the Devil is always lurking and looking for an opportunity to get into my head. I ask all of this in your Son's name. Amen.

That felt good. Prayer has always been important in his life. He had had an ok relationship with God over the years and he knows he needs Him now to help them get through these times. As he has done in the past few days, he poured himself another cup of coffee, and put a few slices of bread into the toaster oven. Opening the fridge he found some strawberry preserves to put on the toasted bread. He spotted an apple and an orange which he took out, cleaned the apple and peeled the orange. He was thankful for whatever he could find to eat when the family was not here. He prayed again out loud "Lord thanks for putting this wonderful family in our lives. Without their support and help I don't know where we would be. But again thanks to you for giving us the strength to overcome the many obstacles that have confronted us. Also thanks for another beautiful day with the sun shining and making things a bit easier to deal with. Continue to watch over Pat and Juan Carlos and that they will continue their journey without trouble. Amen."

After eating the fruit and the bread at the kitchen table, he remembered that Fernando had bought a book for him to read so he hunted in the living area and then the dining room and found it on the entry room table. He thumbed thru the book and he recognized some of the stories he had read either as teenager or a young adult. Initially there were two stories that he had a vague recollection of: The Gold Bug, which was a mystery that included some sort of word puzzles, or codes, and a poem that he remembered memorizing in high school. The poem was called Anabelle Lee. The morning was moving rather slowly so he selected one or two stories to read from the book The first one was "The Pit and The Pendulum and the second one was" The Cask of Amontillado". He read the first one, finished it and began the second one. In the middle of the 2nd story he dozed off. After awakening, what seemed like just a short time, he awoke, looked at the kitchen clock and to his surprise he had slept for almost three hours. Tension and anxiety can often lead to the need for more than normal sleep time. Without question Chris was tense and anxious with all that he had faced and the concern what the future held for he and Pat.

Feeling a bit drowsy, even though he had a long nap, he looked in the fridge again for something to eat for lunch. He noticed that there was a plate of leftover Paella so he put the Paella into a baking dish he found on a shelf and put it into the oven to heat it up. After Chris finished it and combined with a bottle of beer, the Paella even tasted better than the first time he had eaten it the other evening. Culinary experts have always claimed that Paella tasted better when eaten as a leftover. Pasta the same.

CHAPTER SIXTEEN

Chris picked up the Poe book and finished the 2nd story. He enjoyed both stories so he decided to read The Gold Bug that he remembered reading as a young person. He always had a fascination with codes so this story appealed to him. It was a good read and the story was about cryptographs which was another word for coding. The afternoon had flown by and it wouldn't be too long before the family returned to await a call from Juan Carlos in Madrid. Chris tested himself to see if he could recite the poem Anabelle Lee, that he had memorized in High School. He did a pretty good job he thought: "It was many and many a year ago in a kingdom by the sea that maiden there lived by the name of Anabelle Lee. She was a child and I was a child in this kingdom by the sea and we lived with a love that was more than a love I and my Anabelle Lee with a love that winged Seraphs of Heaven coveted her and me." Not the best but he was pleased with himself that he could remember any of it. Good for him. He looked at the clock and it read 4:30PM which meant that Carolina would be home in less than an hour. He was most anxious to see the return of Fernando and Ignacio and the phone call from Madrid.

As per usual, a bit after 5, the front door opened and he heard Carolina yell "Ola Senor Chris" which he knew by then meant hello. He did not answer her hoping she would think that he was taking a nap. He rested a bit and it was not long before the front door opened again and he was certain that it was Ignacio and Fernando. He heard Fernando yell "Chris" and Chris answered saying he would be down in a few minutes. He got to thinking that, even though it seemed like he was not eating well, he had probably gained a few pounds. Having not exercised at all over the past few days, he did feel a bit lethargic. Hopefully this mess will clear up and Pat and he would be back home in their normal routines which include the gym for him and tennis for Pat.

The 7PM hour was almost here and, with that, the call that Fernando said would be coming from Juan Carlos. Unlike the past few nights, Carolina did not offer any wine or cheese and all of them sat in the living area without much of any conversation. He could feel the anxiety and apprehension taking over him as he waited for the news from Spain. He noticed that all of them kept their eyes on the clock on the mantle probably praying for the clock to turn 7. The phone rang and the sound seemed louder than usual which made Chris twitch a bit. Fernando answered it and said " Ola Juan Carlos. Que paso, senor?" After a few seconds he turned to the rest of us and said "It is Juan Carlos on the phone and I will repeat our conversation in its entirety in English for you, Chris, and in Spanish for Ignacio and Carolina."

After listening to Fernando's part in the conversation Chris had no idea what was being said since it was in Spanish. He was losing his patience while waiting for a pause in the conversation so that Fernando could repeat it to them. It seemed like forever but eventually Fernando hung up the phone and began to speak directly to Chris. "Chris, the news is good. Juan says that he and Pat are being well taken care of at the Embassy in Madrid. He said that he has spoken to his cousin, the General, several times in order to be certain about the plan to get Pat and you out of Germany and back home. Here is the plan, almost word for word, from Juan Carlos. The General has talked to Herr Hitler a number of times and the two have devised the following plan. Hitler has no desire to keep you, Chris, and Pat hostage in Germany so he has agreed to help you to leave this country. The General is making his private plane available to fly Juan Carlos and Pat back to Berlin tomorrow morning so that you and Pat will be reunited. Herr Hitler will be sending a driver here to this house sometime around 1 to 2 PM. tomorrow. The driver will take you and I to meet the plane that is coming from Madrid with Pat and Juan Carlos aboard. Juan Carlos thinks it would be best if I accompany you to the airport as a precaution as I am the go between you and the pilots of the plane coming from Madrid. The plane will land here and Hitler is providing a compliment of security people to make sure that neither you nor Pat nor Juan Carlos are disturbed by any of the officials at the airport. Upon arrival the pilots will park the plane, stay overnight and be ready to fly all three of you back to Madrid early in the morning. The pilots will tell me the time they will leave for Madrid tomorrow and the security people will make sure that the 3 of you get to the airport on time for the flight to Madrid. This means that you and Pat will be the guest of Herr Hitler at a Hotel convenient to the airport and, of course, Juan Carlos will be provided with a room of his own. I will also be provided with a room so that I will be with you until your plane leaves Berlin and then I will return home. Since tomorrow is Saturday, I do not have to work and the next day, the day you leave for Madrid, I have no work that day either. You and Pat will spend tomorrow evening at a Hotel in Madrid. The next morning the General has arranged for you to fly commercially to New York City where you will be greeted by customs officials, and by representatives of your President Roosevelt. They will provide transportation to get you and Pat to your home in New Jersey."

"I hope I have explained all of this to you so that there is no misunderstanding of the events to follow. This plan, which involves a number of people here in Berlin and in Madrid needs to strictly follow the time line. I will now give the details to Carolina and her husband. When I finish, I will answer any questions that you have. At this point I know as much as you know.

It took a few minutes for Fernando to share this information with Carolina and Ignacio. By the smiles on their faces Chris could tell that they were pleased with what they were told. "Thank you all for the support you have given to myself and my wife" Chris said. "Without your help this could never have happened. I realize that there are a bunch of people to thank for all the help. I am taken back by who the primary helpers are, Hitler and Franco. When we get home and we tell the story I am sure that most people would find it remarkable who was involved in our getting to leave Germany. I have no questions at this time but perhaps over the next few hours I might have a question or two."

Carolina told Fernando that she would cook a special meal for us but first we need to send a prayer to God for all the blessings He has provided for you, Pat and Juan Carlos. He understood the word Dios which meant God and he heard the names of the 3 of them and when he saw Fernando cross himself he figured out that a prayer would be said. He bowed his head and listened to Carolina recite a prayer in Spanish, and, when she was finished, they all crossed themselves so he did the same so as to acknowledge the prayer. Being a cradle Episcopalian and being a communicant in a High Episcopal Church, displaying the sign of the Cross was second nature to him.

As per usual, Fernando and Ignacio went into the kitchen and returned to the living area with cheese, crackers and white wine. As he had said previously, this routine was becoming a possible tradition for him as, he thought perhaps doing this when they get home. It was good to think of getting home safely as it appears that things would work out to that end. He was feeling more than a bit overjoyed that the ending was no doubt in sight. The 4 of them relished the wine and cheese and, while they were finishing up the wine and cheese, Carolina excused herself saying "con permiso" which he was able to translate as "excuse me".

The dinner meal consisted of Spanish Rice, pan, and a most delicious chicken dish. She also served a salad of huge tomatoes and large slices of white onion. After resting a bit at the dining room table, Carolina went to the kitchen and returned with a pie for dessert and coffee. After dessert he asked to say a word of thanks to Fernando and his family and would he translate into Spanish for them. He shook his head as to agree so Chris said" I cannot put into words the extent of my thanks to all of you. Without your support, there is no way we would be in such a good place with the real hope of returning safely home. You have opened up your home to us, fed us and made us feel safe. I truly understand the risks that you have taken and I humbly and sincerely offer a great sense of gratitude to all that you have done. It appears now that this will be the last night that I will spend in your home and in the morning we will be saying "adios" to each other. With Fernando's help, I offer prayer to all of you; Vaya con dios!" Hugs all around as Fernando translated Chris's prayer and then off to bed for all of them.

Sleep came fairly easy for Chris as so much of the pressure has now been lifted. Tomorrow would bring Pat and he together again. He knew they owed a great deal of gratitude to Juan Carlos for the part that he has played throughout this ordeal. Chris needed to put away all doubts about Pat and Juan Carlos and think very positively about the days to come.

The clock on the end table showed 7:45 when he awoke the next morning. He really felt refreshed but a bit anxious about the events that would take place over the next few days. He wanted to remember everything that Fernando had translated from Juan Carlos. It all sounded so very simple but he was concerned that something could still go wrong. Be upbeat he told himself as he took a shower and dressed. He chuckled at the realization that his choice of clothing was limited to what he wore leaving the Hotel or the attire the family provided for him. So, he decided to mix and match the two sets of clothing so that he would feel like he had a new outfit on. Would anyone of authority notice?

Chris was reminded that Juan Carlos had said a car was coming for Fernando and himself sometime after noon. He rushed down the stairs to greet this wonderful family and enjoy a breakfast with them and some good conversation until it was time to leave. It was Saturday and so they would not be heading for work today.

All were gathered in the dining area and he could smell the aroma of pastry, sausage, and freshly brewed coffee and quickly greeted everyone and took his usual seat at the table. Fernando, in Spanish and in English, said the blessing. Chris thought that the reason why they had not said a blessing at any of the meals they had shared together was because they were not sure he was a Christian. All doubts were removed when he joined them in prayer last night and crossed himself. It felt good to share in the blessing. He was pretty quiet during breakfast as he was busy feeding his face with the wonderful food. He probably ate too much but what of it. The family talked a bit in Spanish and he was pleased that he could understand a word here and there. Wouldn't it be nice to learn another language, perhaps Spanish, after he got home.

After eating he excused himself saying "Con permiso" and went to his room to freshen up, rest a bit and to say goodbye to the bedroom he had slept in the past few nights. Although not large by standards at home, it was most comfortable. There was no need to pack a suitcase as there was nothing to put in it. However he noticed the razor and shaving cup on the sink and would ask them if he could take this with him as a reminder of their wonderful hospitality.

He checked the bedside clock and it said 10:55 which meant that they would be leaving for the airport in just a few hours. He walked down the stairs, shaving stuff in his hands, and walked into the living area where all were seated. He told Fernando to say to Carolina that he was sorry that he did not help cleaning up after breakfast. He laughed a bit as did the others when translated into Spanish. He also explained why he had the shaving stuff with him. Carolina and Ignacio said that it would be ok for him to keep.

While sitting there wishing the time away Carolina brought some fruit and cheese into the living area. It was now close to noon and the car would be arriving at any moment. He was not that hungry but it would be rude if he did not eat a bit. Also he had no idea when he would eat again.

It was not very long before the doorbell rang and Fernando went to answer the door. After a brief time he came back into the living area accompanied by two men who were dressed in formal military uniforms. He said "These are two of Hitler's representatives who will take us to the airport to await the arrival of the plane from Madrid and there are two more in the car outside. I think it is time for us to leave, so say your goodbyes to Carolina and Ignacio, and we will be on our way".

Chris hugged Carolina and Ignacio and they hugged back. He was getting a bit emotional but held back the tears. They both said in Spanish" Goodbye and have a safe trip back home. Please tell your wife that we are praying for you both".

Accompanied by Fernando and the two soldiers, Chris left the home and was seated in this huge Mercedes Benz that had three rows of seats. A few minutes after they left Fernando spoke to the soldier sitting in the front passenger seat. Chris had no idea what the conversation was all about and after quite a lengthy conversation Fernando turned to him and said" You remember what Juan Carlos said about Hitler's sending his people to protect all of us once we get to the airport." He continued "They will be with us until you, Pat and Juan Carlos leave tomorrow morning to go to Madrid. He tells me that the plane from Spain will be arriving at about 4PM this afternoon so we will be taken to a private area to await the arrival. Do you have any questions?" He answered him "Thanks for the information. I do have one request. Is it possible for me to purchase a change of clothes while we await the plane? I have been wearing the same clothing for about 4 days. I think I would like a change. I only have about 200 marks left." Fernando said that he would talk to the soldiers to see if that might be possible but he had no idea what one can buy with those marks but he would see.

Upon arriving at the airport they were taken to a private room. Shortly afterwards a soldier came into the room with sandwiches, soft drinks and some pastries. Fernando and Chris, obviously, were very hungry since they had not eaten anything or drank anything since earlier this morning. Fernando, in German, thanked the soldiers for the food and drinks.

Chris asked Fernando again about his buying new clothes at the airport. He said that he had talked to them but they told him that there wasn't a store near here. After about 30 minutes, another soldier came into the room and spoke to Fernando. Fernando said" I have been told that the plane has landed earlier than expected and they will take us to meet the plane out on the field" Chris's heart started to beat faster as he prepared to see Pat exit from the plane where he would greet her and Juan Carlos. When they got to the plane several people were walking down the staircase. Chris watched and waited but no Pat. He did see Juan Carlos get off the plane so he went over to the staircase to ask where Pat was.

After a bit of thought Juan Carlos said" Well, she got off the plane before I did and told me she would see us in the terminal. Didn't you see her when you were walking to the plane?" He said no they did not see her and, without hesitation, Chris ran frantically into the terminal. It was Sunday and the terminal was almost empty but there were no sign of Pat.

Fernando joined Chris continuing looking for Pat. After a while they noticed that Juan Carlos was no longer with them. No doubt he was looking for Pat in another part of the terminal. Fernando suggested that they go back to the private room they were in and he would ask the soldiers to try and find Pat giving them a complete description. After several hours the soldiers told them that they looked everywhere but could not find her. Fernando asked the soldiers if they had seen Juan Carlos, who he had described. They all said no. Chris was in a panic. What is going on here? Someone must have seen them. After the news of not finding them Fernando and Chris decided to go back into the terminal and try to find Pat and Chris. They searched and searched, asking those they ran into if they had seen either Pat or Juan Carlos but they had no luck. By that time it was almost dark. Fernando said to Chris" Tomorrow is Monday and I will need to go home now and be ready to go to work tomorrow. I am sorry that I can't stay with you much longer. I think the best thing to do would be for me to accompany you back to the hotel where you will again spend the night and tomorrow you can continue the hunt for Pat and Juan Carlos. I have spoken with the soldiers and they agreed to continue to guard you and to continue to look for those missing. They also said that a higher up official, who is fluent in English, will meet you for breakfast in the dining area at 8AM."

They walked back to the Hotel, to the stairs up to their room where Fernando gave Chris a big hug and wished him good luck. He also said that Herr Hitler was aware of the current situation and that, relayed to me by one of the soldiers, he would continue to informed of progress in the hours ahead.

After Fernando left, the panic that Chris felt seemed to ramp up to the point that he could not think clearly at all. Here he was, completely alone at a hotel at the airport in Berlin, not being able to converse with the soldiers that were guarding him as he knew no German. He opened the room door, walked out, motioned to one of the soldiers by putting his fingers next to his mouth hoping that he would understand that he was hungry. The guard understood because he made the same motion with a broad smile on his face and said "Ya Ya" as he ushered Chris back into his room. He left but returned in about one half hour with a tray of sandwiches and a pot of coffee and, of course, some pastries. Chris said to himself that the Germans sure eat a lot of pastries. He bowed his head to him as a gesture of thanks and, after he left, Chris began to dig into what the soldier brought him.

After dinner he took a shower and tried to relax but he

continued to try and come to some understanding of what happened to his wife and Juan Carlos. The more he thought the more he panicked. He needed to get hold of himself, get some sleep and await some good news in the morning. He slept fitfully but managed a few hours of sleep. He awoke in the morning hearing a loud knock on his door. He jumped out of bed, opened the door and the soldier that brought him the food last night greeted him "Guten tag Herr Casey". He then pointed to his watch which said 7:30 and he also made the gesture of eating. He was reminding him that someone who spoke English was to meet Chris for breakfast in the Hotel dining room, So Chris said "Danka" and closed the door. He still had the shaving gear with him so he showered, shaved and got dressed and left the room accompanied by the soldiers who led him to the dining room.

The man he was introduced to by one of the soldiers was dressed in an all black military uniform with lightening bolts on both sides of the collar. Since Chris knew he could speak English he said to him, as he sat down," I desperately need your help". Before he could say another word, the German said" My name is Colonel Franz Gutenstaffen. I am a senior officer in the SS corps of our military. I have been advised of your situation since yesterday afternoon and I have been working on trying to find your wife and your friend Juan Carlos. I have good news and bad news. The good news is that I have located them in a nearby hotel but the bad news, I assume, is that they are registered as man and wife, Senor and Senora Juan Carlos. I will take you to them as we have not allowed them to leave their room. We do not understand what is going on here. Why are they registered as man and wife. Perhaps you can shed some light on the matter"

Needless to say Chris was shocked to hear that Pat and Juan Carlos were still acting as man and wife. Perhaps, before he got really upset, it was a ploy to get them back to Berlin and then both Pat and he would be given new passports to get them home. He told the German officer that he had no idea what was happening. He could not explain their continuing to pose as man and wife. Chris asked to be taken to the hotel room where they were and, after some conversation, he could explain the whole situation. Even though Chris was anxious to see Pat, he was also quite hungry. He asked if they could put the meeting off for a bit while he ate breakfast and thought about the meeting with Pat and Juan Carlos.

After a very filling German breakfast that included different kinds of sausage, some local fruit and strong coffee, the Colonel signed the check and asked Chris to follow him to his car. The car, a huge Mercedes Benz, was parked at the entrance of the Hotel and they sat in the backseat. The Colonel, in German, gave the driver instructions to take them to the Hotel where Pat and Juan Carlos were staying. It was a very short ride and Chris followed the Colonel out of the car into the hotel, up the elevator to the third floor, where they exited, and walked down the hall to Room 322. Chris was impressed by the opulence of the hotel. It was in grand style similar to most of the buildings he had seen in Berlin much more elegant than the one he had been in. As he stood in front of the Room 322 there were two German military seated with side arms in chairs blocking the door. His heart began to race preparing him for what would happen next.

The Colonel knocked on the door and asked Chris to step aside while he entered the room alone. Chris thought this most peculiar but did not wish to argue with him. It just served to push his anxiety level to a new high. What would he find out when he sees Pat. In a few minutes the Colonel opened the door, then closed it and told Chris he would bring him to another room where Pat would meet him. Again Chris thought this most upsetting as all kinds of thoughts ran through his mind. He was led to a room several doors from Room 322. The numbers on the door was 326. He walked into the room which appeared to have a bedroom, a bathroom and a fairly large size sitting room. The room was furnished with what obviously was expensive furniture with elegant paintings adorning the walls. There were fresh flowers on the sideboard. Chris stepped into the room and could see on the other side of the room a door that led to an outside patio that overlooked the city. Chris began to pace up and down nervously as he tried to calm himself, needing to relax prior to his meeting with Pat and Juan Carlos.

After a few minutes there was knock on the door. He ran to the door and opened it and there was his lovely wife standing there. He threw his arms around her, welcoming her with tears running down his face. Pat did not seem to be as happy to see him as he was to see her. He tried to kiss her but she turned away and walked into the room while Chris shut the door. "Pat, I am so happy to see you and to see that you are safe. We have been apart for only a few days but it seems more like weeks. I know that you have probably been concerned about my welfare as well but apparently you and Juan Carlos were being informed as to my situation. Is that right? Tell me what you can about how you have spent the past few days. I know that you and Juan Carlos flew to Spain aided by the Spanish Embassy in Berlin. I also know that because of Juan Carlos's position you had the assistance of both General Franco in Spain and also Adolph Hitler here in Germany. Tell me how you are. Are you ok? Are you ill? You seem a bit detached. Can you tell me if there is a problem that I am not aware of. I so want to get the both of us back home as soon as possible so help me" Chris was confused and hoped Pat could help him understand what had happened since their last goodbye and would get them home.

Pat said "I am so glad to see you and that you are well and that you have not suffered during our being apart. Everything that you were told in Berlin by Fernando is pretty much the story of Juan Carlos and my journey till now. No question that I was very anxious about what would happen to us but, when Juan Carlos told me who he was and how he was connected to the Spanish leader, I felt considerably more at ease. The plan was for Juan and myself to fly back to Berlin where you and I would be united, fly the three of us back to Madrid and then for you and I to fly home. It is true that this plan was made possible by both the General and Hitler. The passport I have is issued in the name of Patricia Fortunato, traveling as the wife of Juan Carlos, in order that there would be no problem in my coming and going from Berlin to Madrid and back again to Berlin. Later on this afternoon the three of us will fly to Madrid. The Spanish Embassy here in Berlin, with the help of the US Consulate, has issued a new passport to allow you to fly back to the States from Madrid in the morning. I will not be joining you as I have decided to stay in Madrid with Juan Carlos. I know what I am about to say will be a great shock to you but I have made my decision after a great deal of thought and I will not change my mind."

Pat went on to say" From the moment I met Juan Carlos there was this intense sexual arousal. I don't think it had anything to do with our sex life but it was inescapable. The more time I was around him the desire became stronger. When we were at last alone at the Spanish Embassy, before flying to Madrid, we both admitted to each other the feelings we had for each other. We slept together that night and have continued to be sexually active with each other ever since. What has happened goes against everything that I know and understood about marriage; you know the wedding vows. I have tried to convince myself that this was only a brief fling but, as the days go on, it has become a reality for me. I realize how this decision I have made will affect, not only you but our kids back home. I am certain that you will all go on with your lives without me."

As Pat went on, the tears were rolling down his face and he felt a sick feeling in his stomach. Is this a dream but he soon realized that it was not. After many years of marriage, where there was never a question of infidelity on either part, it really rocked his world. He was half hearing what she was saying and half thinking about how he could respond. " Chris, I wish this had never happened but it has and we both need to deal with the reality of this situation. Because of the conflict that has begun in Europe, Juan Carlos has convinced me that the United States would soon be involved and that it would be safer for me to be in Spain. He has convinced me that Hitler and Germany will prevail even if the US , England and France become involved. Because of his position in the Spanish government and the good relationship the General has with Hitler, my decision to live in Spain is what I want. Juan has told me that the official status of Spain is to be non-belligerent and intended to express sympathy, economic and military support for Germany and Italy".

Chris sensed that she was awaiting some response from him but he was in a state of shock. He almost lost his balance as he moved towards one of the comfortable over stuffed chairs in the room sitting down and trying to pull himself together. He asked Pat to sit in the chair next to his. Chris began "Needless to say, I'm shocked and angry hearing your story. I can't believe that this has happened in such a short time. I thought our marriage was on a solid foundation, especially after all that, as a family, we went through because of the depression. There was never, in my mind, a time when I had reservations about our relationship. As I sit and think of how to respond, my first thought is that I love you and will always love you and I will not take your decision as a finality. Over the past week our lives have been in a state of both confusion and despair due to what is happening in Europe. I do believe that Juan Carlos is right when he says that the United States will enter the war shortly but I disagree completely with the thought that Hitler could overcome the will and power of France, England and the US. But that is not the important thing here. The important thing for me is to convince you that even though you have been unfaithful to me, because of the circumstances surrounding your infidelity, I am willing to continue our marriage as it has been and for us to return together to the States."

"We have both been under tremendous pressure and I believe this pressure has had a very negative influence on you in particular. To my mind, I cannot conceive that you want to change your entire life as it existed prior to our trip to Europe. Based on your explanation as to what was to occur over the next 48 hours, I am not going to go away easily and I am determined to convince you to change your mind. If nothing else I believe you need to give me a chance to get you to change your mind and to come home with me" As he finished he broke down and cried in an almost convulsive way and waited for Pat to respond.

As he looked up at her he could see her eyes welling up and a few tears rolling down her face. "Chris" she said" I am so sorry to hurt you in this way. At this time I do understand what I will be giving up in staying in Spain with Juan Carlos but I have mulled this over and over again over the past few days and am still of the same frame of mind. Perhaps you are correct when you say how things like this could happen in such a short period of time and how my decision has been made in the midst of some very trying circumstances. I too have factored all of this into my choice and am still convinced to stay in Spain."

Still in a virtual state of shock Chris needed to pull himself together and to formulate a line of thinking that would get Pat to change her mind so he said" Pat I am trying to understand how and for what reasons you have made this decision but you must give me the opportunity to convince you otherwise. Since it is still early in the day, please, please convince Juan Carlos and whoever you need to, that you need one more day to think about your staying in Spain. Here is what I suggest. Ask Juan Carlos to postpone the trip for the three of us to go to Madrid for 24 hours. That done, would you spend the rest of the day with me and after diner, we go to separate rooms and that you consider seriously changing your decisions. I don't want to say that you owe me at least this chance but I do want to say that you owe our marriage the opportunity to be 100% sure about your decision. I will leave you in this room for 30 minutes or so and come back to hopefully hear that you will agree to my wish" Pat thought a minute and agreed to think about his plan for the rest of the day. Chris got up and walked towards the door, looked back at Pat, who he could see was in tears, and he left the room.

Outside the door the Colonel was waiting for him and Chris knew he wanted to know what was going on. He explained to him that he was to return to this room in 30 minutes to resume his conversation with his wife. Chris told him that he would like to spend 30 minutes by himself and to point out where he would have his privacy. Chris followed him to the staircase and down to the first floor whereupon they entered the dining area. It was about 11AM and it was not crowded. The Colonel took him to a table far in the rear of the restaurant and said" This is a very quiet place. If you wish you may order something to drink or eat and I will be back in about 45 minutes and I will sign the check "and with that he left.

Chris looked around and saw no one close by. A waiter approached his table and Chris ordered coffee. He was back shortly with a tray of coffee, cream, sugar and pastries. As he started to eat a pastry and relish the hot coffee he was jolted into reality as he saw Juan Carlos heading towards him. He said "Please excuse me but we need to talk". Chris said to him "There is nothing to talk about with him." He went on further to say "My wife and I will discuss the matter and there was no need for me to talk with you." He could see that Chris was very angry and chose to walking away. All Chris could think of was that he wanted to beat the hell out of that man but realized that it would only complicate the situation. What kind of nerve would someone like that have to confront him. Maybe the Europeans have a different standard than we do in matters of the heart.

He spent the time allotted thinking of how he was going to change Pat's mind. The only thing that made sense was to convince her of two things. One was to help her understand that her safety would be at risk if she stayed in Europe and especially in Spain being involved with someone who was sympathetic with Hitler and that the involvement of the US in the war would lead to defeat of Hitler's plans for Germany. Two, he would remind her of not only her obligations to her children back home but the fact that he loved her very much and was concerned for her safety. This was the plan and he prayed that it would work. The Colonel came to get him as he said he would. Chris told him that he should not have told Juan Carlos where he was since they had nothing to talk about. The Colonel did not offer an apology and motioned for him to follow. Returning to the room where Pat had spent the time in solitude, he was anxious to begin to make his case. She turned to him and said "Why did you turn away from a conversation with Juan Carlos?" Chris told her he did not choose to talk to him and that the matter was between them.

No question that at this point both of them were exhausted from the stress they were both going through. He asked her if she wanted something to eat or drink and she replied" Thanks for asking. Perhaps some black coffee". He went to the door, opened it and asked one of the guards for some coffee and he said something in German that Chris did not understand. However he must have understood Chris because he was back in about ten minutes with a pot of coffee, some cream and sugar and two cups. Chris thanked the soldier "Danka" and poured the coffee for himself and for Pat.

Chris hesitated and the words did not come easily in response to the situation that he and Pat found themselves. Before he could speak, Pat said that Juan Carlos had changed the plan and that they would go tomorrow instead of today to Madrid. This is what Chris hoped for so that Pat would have the time to reassess her decision to stay in Europe.

Chris, with a lump in his throat and an ache in his heart, he spoke" Pat, we have been together since high school just 2 kids that had fallen in love. No one knows me better than you do and no one knows you better than I do. Would you try and reflect back on all the good times and the struggle times we had over the years especially during the depression when you went back to teaching because our family needed the money? Remember the difficult choices we had to make about what we would be able to do financially that impacted the whole family. The kids were too young to completely understand our needing to pull back on events and planned activities. We thought all of this out together and it made our marriage stronger and also our love for each other grew. Other than both of us losing our tempers from time to time we really never had an argument that lasted more than overnight. Try and remember, when we first fell in love, what it was that made you love me. I will admit that our sex life was not as robust as you probably would have liked and I will take the blame for that. It could not have been too bad as we have two wonderful children to show for it. I know that my work involved spending a lot more time and energy on the job but my sense was that I was providing a good life for you and the children. That was my choice and, from my point of view, I wanted the very best for you and the kids. Thankfully my career enabled all that I dreamed about for the family to come true. Promotions afforded good increases in our income and the results speak for themselves. No question that I should have been there more so for you and the kids but I was not and I am sad if you in some way hold that against me. I desperately need you and the children need you to remain part of this family as it now exists. I don't think that either one of us could explain your decision to them. It is difficult enough for me come to grips with your decision. They are 18 and 19 with Sam being a sophomore and Laura beginning her first year in college. The plan was for them to be off to school when we got home. The shock of your not coming home and your not being there for them would be immense. Please, please think about all this and consider the consequences of your leaving versus your staying. I am concerned about your safety staying here in Europe and in Spain. There is no doubt in my mind that when the US enters the war, eventually we will bring Hitler to his knees which in turn will have a major impact on Spain and General Franco and to all members of his government. You need to consider all I have said and tomorrow tell me that you have changed your mind and will come home with me" As he finished the tears began again and he was all chocked up. All he could do now was to pray for a good outcome.

CHAPTER SEVENTEEN

Pat appeared to listen and hear what he was saying which gave him a sense of accomplishment. Her answer was short and to the point. She said" I still have strong feelings for you and I need to consider what my defection, so to speak, from our family would mean to all concerned. I listened attentively to all that you said and I know it came from the heart. I will do as you suggest and will have an answer for you at the airport when we plan to fly to Madrid and then together home or you by yourself". Pat got up, looked a bit shaky, and left the room they were in. So, he would know tomorrow what her final decision will be and can only pray for her to come home.

Chris went back to his room, and before entering he asked one of the soldiers to ask Colonel Gutenstaffen to come to his room. Guess they understood because one of them left and came back shortly with the Colonel. Chris asked him where he could have dinner. He said to him" I will take you to the dining room but before I do I need to know what is going on with you, your wife and the gentleman from Madrid." Chris's response was that the three of them would be taking the plane back to Madrid tomorrow morning. He also asked what time would he need to be ready to leave for the airport. He told him that his wife and Juan Carlos will be meeting him at the plane. The Colonel said "I will let you know the details when I meet you at the restaurant and sign your dinner charges. Give me an hour and I will meet you there"

Chris followed him to the restaurant. It seemed more crowded than the other times he had eaten there. He noticed, as he was shown to his table, that there was an unusual number of German officers who were eating there. He could not understand what they were saying but they sure sounded happy as they seemed to toast each other with beer steins. The Colonel spoke to the waiter in German and Chris assumed he told him that he would be back in an hour to sign for my meal.

Since he could not read the menu he asked the Colonel, as he had done before, to translate the menu so he could order. Chris selected a lentil soup, a garden salad, brisket, mashed potatoes and green beans. He also asked him to order some bread and some coffee for after the meal.

As he waited for his food he thought back on the conversation that he had with Pat. He prayed quietly that God would support him and have Pat make the right decision. He knew that there is nothing he could do at this point and it was up to the Lord to do his thing as He is always in control. The noise from the Germans who seemed to be in celebration continued and soon the waiter came with his soup and some bread. He bowed and said" Danka ". Chris had noticed that people in Berlin seemed to bow to each other as a token of respect so when in Rome do as the Romans do. The salad came and shortly after the waiter returned with the main course. He was tired and he was filled with anxiety but he enjoyed the entire meal. As he waited for the Colonel he drank several cups of coffee which he regretted later that evening. The Colonel arrived and signed the check. He sat next to Chris and said something to the waiter who shortly came with coffee for the Colonel. "These are your instructions for tomorrow,' said the Colonel. Be ready to leave at about 8:30. There will not be time for breakfast but they will serve you something on the plane. I have been told that your wife and Juan Carlos, as you said, will meet you on the plane. I will escort you to your room and I will meet you in the lobby at 8:30 in the morning. I trust you will have a pleasant sleep". So off they went to his room and they said their goodnights and Chris prepared for sleep. He was tired but could not fall asleep immediately. He never had a problem falling asleep but all that was going on and the coffee kept him awake. He did remember to set the wind up clock alarm for 7:30 which would give him plenty of time to be in the lobby at 8:30.

CHAPTER EIGHTEEN

The alarm rang and he lazily got out of bed feeling like he had not slept at all but he knew that his emotions were creating problems for him so he did not worry about lack of sleep. He took a shower, and when he looked over at the same old clothes that he had been wearing for about a week, he thought about getting back home and putting all of this behind him. Before getting dressed he looked on the shelf in the bathroom and saw the only possessions that he had. His toothbrush, toothpaste and his shaving gear that Carolina's family had supplied him with, so he brushed his teeth and shaved and then put all of that into a paper bag that he assumed was to be used for laundry.

It was now 8:45 and he opened his room door, hopefully for the last time, and there were the 2 guards that had been present yesterday. He wondered if they had to stayed all night or did someone relieve them. Who cares. He was on his way home from Germany and on his way home hopefully with Pat. He bowed to them and took the stairs down to the lobby where the Colonel was waiting for him. He looked all around hoping to see Pat but she was not there but he remembered that the Colonel said they would meet him on the plane.

They left the hotel and made their way to what looked like the same official car he rode in yesterday. The Colonel sat next to him and said that it would be a very short ride to the airport. The trip from the airport to the hotel would be the reverse today. There was no conversation so he sat back and tried his best to relax. He felt like his heart was beating 200 times a minute and the sense of continuing anxiety overtook him. Soon he would I know if Pat was coming with him. He felt really good about the chances of her coming as he had made a good case for her changing her mind. He tried to recall what time the plane would leave for Madrid. He thought 11:00 o'clock so he asked the Colonel and he confirmed the 11AM time.

They arrived at the airport at about 9:30 and the Colonel took him to a private room which Chris thought was the room he was in several days ago. He spoke to one of guards stationed outside the room and told him it would be a while so he ordered some coffee and some pastries to have while waiting. Chris thanked him but he was not certain that he would be able to drink the coffee much less eat the pastries. It did not take long and the German soldier brought a tray of coffee and pastries with 2 cups and 2 plates into the room. The aroma got to him so he decided to drink the coffee and ate a bit of one of the pastries. After a while the door opened and one of the soldiers whispered something into the Colonel's ear. " It is time to go to board the plane ,so please follow me. They walked through the terminal and, as they did, he looked and looked for Pat but there was no sign of her.

The Colonel led him out of the Terminal to the area where a number of planes were parked. Most of the planes had what looked like German military insignias stenciled on the tail section. They seemed to be the only ones in the area and, as they walked a bit further, he noticed a plane smaller than the German planes with the word Espana stenciled on the side of the plane. He guessed Espana meaning Spain and he knew he was right as the Colonel led him to a staircase going up to the front of the plane. He proceeded him up the stairs, walked into the cabin with Chris behind him. Chris looked into the cabin, turned towards the seats, and it was completely empty. Where was Pat? Why isn't she here? He led him to one of the seats at the front of the cabin and asked to make himself comfortable. Chris had this sick feeling and asked him "Where is my wife?" He paused for a moment and then said "If she is coming she will be here in just a few minutes" "What do you mean if she is coming" Chris said. "I thought you said she would meet me on the plane" He said have patience but if she's not here in 10 minutes, my commanding officer has told me to close the plane door and that the plane would take off to Madrid with only you on it."

The ten minutes flew by and no Pat. The Colonel saluted him, went on to the staircase and closed the door before Chris could reach him. The planes engines began to turn on and the plane slowly moved away from where it was moored. Chris said to himself that he could not believe what had happened. He was not prepared for

Pat not coming but there was not much he could do at this point. The plane continued to slowly move down what appeared to be a runway of sorts and then it turned and gunned its engines as preparation to take off. Instead the pilot apparently slowed down the engines and they did not take off. Chris did not know what to think. Maybe there was a mechanical problem or maybe Pat had arrived at the airport after the plane was in a position to take off. There was no one in the cabin except him so he could not ask anyone what was going on. Since there were no windows, he sensed that the plane was heading back to the area where it was parked when he got on the plane. He could only hope that the reason the plane did not take off was that Pat had arrived late at the airport and they were heading back so she could join him.

After they had parked, he could not see if the staircase had been moved to the front door of the plane but he heard the noise of it hitting the cabin's door. He saw the front door of the plane open and there she was. His prayers had been answered and Pat would be coming home with him. He rushed to greet her, put his arms around her and hugged her with all his might. Something was wrong. "You are not coming with me back home" he said. She replied " I have not given myself enough time to think about this. I need more time so I have decided to stay in Europe, probably Spain, for an extended period of time so that I will have had the time necessary to come to a final decision. It is not that I don't love you and the kids but for the first time in my life I have an important decision to make that will affect the rest of my life. I have called Sam and Laura and have told them that I will be staying here for a time and that you will be coming home alone. I said that I would keep in touch with them at their Colleges and they need not worry about me. I will be fine. Of course, they were shocked, I guess that is the right word, but they seemed to understand what I was saying. I spoke to Juan Carlos and we have decided to live in separate residences in Madrid while I am considering this choice of staying or going back to the US. He has also agreed that he will provide me with housing and will pay for all of the expenses that I will incur while living in Spain and that he will honor my decision whenever I make it."

She continued "I could not let you leave without sharing this with you. In the meantime please take care of yourself and be gentle with the kids as they were not prepared for my not coming home. Since they are both in College with lots to do and with lots of friends, the time will go quickly for them. In the end, I hope that you will give me the time I need to make a choice and that you will not make any rash decisions during the time I am away. I do love you and I am sorry. When you arrive in Madrid you will be met by one of the associates of General Franco. That person will instruct you as to where you will be spending the night and will also be there the next morning to take you to the plane that will take you home. He will provide you with your passport which was obtained from the US Embassy in Madrid. I suppose if you need more help you can contact the Embassy." With that she turned around and moved towards the plane's door.

CHAPTER NINETEEN

Chris started to run after her but stopped half way as he realized no good would come from that. He went back to his seat and saw the door of the plane begin to close and shortly after that the plane began to move to its take off position. Once the plane took off he took a deep breath and settled in his seat. He looked around and , indeed, he was the only one on the plane except for the pilots: hopefully there were two pilots. On second thought God was there as He always is so Chris prayed to Him and asked for some guidance as he has given him in the past. He listened and listened but heard no words from God but he knew that he needed to be patient in hearing from Him just as He is patient in hearing from him. " Help me Lord and tell me what I need to do to retain my sanity and to be able to find a way of life , at least for the foreseeable future, without Pat in my life, at our home? How do I talk to my kids so that they don't feel abandoned by their Mom? Will I be able to assume my new position at the Bank and do the kind of job that the Board expects me to do? With the kids at school what will my days look like coming home at night to a empty house and what about weekends? Lord, there are so many things going through my mind that it is overwhelming. If I feel like that now, what happens when I get home? I need your help which you have always provided me in the past. Which one of my friends will I be able to count on for support and how do I explain the details around Pat's choice? Wow! So much to deal with but first and foremost is my being there for the kids."

Thank goodness he had some coffee and pastries for breakfast as he would be famished by now. There was no one to ask about food and drink except the pilots but he wasn't about to knock on the cockpit door. For sure they did not speak English and he had problems with Spanish although he remembered Bebe (drink) and comida(food) in Spanish. After a while the cockpit door opened and one of the pilots came over to him and said "Hola. Como esta, Senor

Casey. Quiere café y comida? Tenemos albos en la cocina." Chris replied in Spanish" Si! Café y comida por favor" He was proud of myself in asking for what he wanted in Spanish. The pilot nodded to him and went to the rear of the plane. In a bit he brought some black coffee (He was not about to ask for sugar or cream as he had no idea how to say that in Spanish) and some cookies and a bit of what looked like cheese in a wrapper of sorts. Chris said gracias, the pilot nodded again and returned to the cockpit.

The coffee was hot and the cookies and cheese were very much welcomed having no idea how long the flight would be to Madrid. He looked around for something to read but no luck. How could he have read anything as it would no doubt be in Spanish? There were no windows on the plane as there are on commercial planes so he was stuck with nothing to do but reflect on the happenings over the past few days. To him it seemed like many weeks but, in fact, only less than a week.

The plane ride was a bit bumpy but not enough to rattle him. He never could get used to turbulence on a plane but having flown only a few times it really never mattered. He tried to doze off but his mind was racing and he did not sleep at all. After several hours he was aware that the plane was descending which meant they would probably land soon. He recalled that Pat said he would be met at the airport by an official from the Spanish Government but he wondered what next. The landing was ok and in a few moments the plane came to a halt. The plane door slowly opened and in walked a man who was rather well dressed, in his early 40's he thought. He welcomed him to Madrid in his very best English and asked him to follow him. . He still had the bag with the shaving stuff in it so he took it with him. The weather outside was quite nice but a bit on the cool side. He was without a coat and still wearing the same clothes which no doubt smelled a bit by now. Chris followed him a few paces behind to a waiting car that had several flags flown on the front bumpers so he assumed the car was a government vehicle.

Once inside the car the gentleman introduced himself to Chris saying "Good afternoon Senor Casey. Welcome to Madrid. I bid you greetings from General Franco and to tell you that he is sorry he could not meet with you personally. My name is Jose Maria DiSilva and I am to be with you until tomorrow when you will board a plane to take you back to America. We will now make our way to a Hotel where you will be housed until the time to leave for the airport in the morning. I am sure you will find the room to your liking. When you are ready to dine you may pick up the phone and a menu will be brought to you. Select anything you wish and, as I said before, you are a welcome guest of the General."

Arriving at the Hotel Mr. DiSilva motioned for him to follow him to the elevator which took them to the 4th floor. The room that he had been given was directly across from the elevator. He opened the door and, once Chris was inside, he was impressed with the room but not quite as elaborate as the one that Pat was staying in Berlin. Mr. Di Silva said "I know you will be comfortable here and please call when you are ready to eat dinner. I am to give you your new American passport which the American Embassy has sent to you. If you have any questions you may call the Embassy. The phone number is in the passport. Please have a relaxing evening and I will call for you at 8AM in the morning. We will have breakfast together and then I will deliver you to the airport where you will board a Pan American flight to Washington. I bid you good night. Oh, I almost forgot. I was instructed to provide you with a new wardrobe to wear in the morning on the plane. Here is your passport and I wish you a pleasant evening."

Chris began to realize how well he was treated in Berlin and now again in Madrid. He mused that he would gladly give that up if Pat were with him. Wonder why the special treatment and, of course, the reason had to do with Juan Carlos and his position in the government. The room seemed quite comfortable. He decided to check the closet to see what kind of clothing he had been given. On the rack was a blue double breasted jacket, a pair of grey slacks, a white dress shirt and a red tie. On the floor there was a package, which he opened and found a pair of briefs, socks and a pair of what he would call penny loafers. How did they know what sizes he needed? Pat must have told them. He needed a shower and went into the bathroom where he found towels and a bathrobe and pajamas. He undressed, took a long shower, put on the pjs and the robe and called the desk to ask for a menu as he was instructed. Shortly thereafter, a white jacketed waiter came to his room with a menu and

Chris circled what he wanted to eat.

The meal was just ok but it wasn't paella that Carolina served him in Berlin. There was a wind up clock on the bedside table so he set the alarm for 7AM and got into bed. He fell asleep almost immediately and awoke the next morning when the alarm rang. He got up and took his bag with shaving stuff into the bathroom, took another shower and then shaved. He opened the closet and put on the clothing that he had seen last night. Everything, including the shoes, fit him perfectly. It was not long after that he heard a knock on the door and there was Mr. DiSilva. He wished Chris a good morning and motioned for Chris to follow him. They had a light breakfast in the dining area and, when finished, Mr. DiSilva ushered him out of the Hotel into the same car they had taken last night.

There was no conversation on the way to the airport other than Mr. DiSilva saying that he would be met at the airport by a representative from the US Embassy. As they entered the terminal he was introduced to that representative whose name he didn't catch. He said" Good morning Mr. Casey. I will accompany you to your plane and will leave you there. When you arrive in Washington tomorrow you will be met by an aide to Mr. Roosevelt and be taken to the White House in order to debrief you on your time in Germany and in Spain."

Chris said thank you and followed him out to the plane. On the way out he was asked by an agent for his passport which he gave to him. He returned it to Chris after stamping it. They went up the stairs to the plane and he showed him to a seat by a window. Finally in a plane with a window. He wished him well and left. Over the loudspeaker. In English, he was instructed to fasten his seat belt and told that the flight to Washington would take about 8 hours. Since the plane was TWA, the stewardesses were American. One of them led him to the rear of the plane to a seat by himself. The plane appeared only about half full.

CHAPTER TWENTY

The flight to Washington was long but the seat was comfortable and they brought him lunch and asked what he would like to drink. He asked for a beer and they brought him a bottle of Spanish beer. Every once and a while a stewardess would ask him if he needed anything and if he were comfortable. Thank goodness there were some magazines in English that he could read and the time passed quickly with his dozing off from time to time. As the flight continued his anxiety level began to rise again knowing the many questions his friends and kids would be asking him.

Upon landing at the airport in Washington, the plane taxied to an area close to the terminal. Over the loud speaker one of the crew told them to remain in their seats until the no smoking sign went off and they would then be parked at the terminal. Chris was able to look out the window to see the gate being pushed to the door. The door opened and, as he moved with the other passengers to the doorway, there stood a man with a large card with his name on it. Chris said "I am Mr. Casey" He shook his hand and said I am Peter Foxworthy. I will be taking you to the White House where you will be questioned by several officials and the President will also be there. Do you have any luggage?" Chris said "I have no luggage except for the small bag I am carrying."

As they walked down the stairs, he was excited to be back in the States recalling all that he had gone through over the past week. He was escorted to a waiting limo which took them to the White House. As they arrived there they came to a gate where there was a sentry post with 2 Marines on duty. Mr. Foxworthy motioned for him to get out of the car and to follow him to the sentry post. It was obvious that the Marines knew Mr. Foxworthy who whispered something to one of them. "Sir, may I see your passport" the Marine asked: Did you bring anything with you off the plane? If you did you need to let me look at whatever you have and to also search you".

Chris told them that he only had a bag containing his shaving stuff which he handed to the Marine. The search took only a few minutes whereupon Mr. Foxworthy motioned for Chris to please get back in the car. They made kind of a circular course which ended under a Porte cashier where they exited the car and entered through some French doors into the building. Chris was led to an elevator which they entered and he could feel the elevator going down. He thought how exciting this was to be in the White House for the first time. The elevator stopped and Chris followed him down the hallway to a set of double doors which was being guarded by two Marines. They opened the door and, as Chris walked into the room, he saw a large table with a group of Military guys seated along with a few men in suits. He was led to the very end of the table where he was asked to make himself comfortable.

The sight of the large group made him somewhat uncomfortable feeling as if he had done something wrong and would be given the third degree. After a brief time one of the suits said "Welcome to the White House Mr. Casey... My name is Roger Cashman. I am the Chief officer in charge of The Information Agency. Please relax as we will be asking you about the last few days you and your wife spent in Berlin. We have compiled a dossier on you and your wife which includes information about your business career and your personal life. I must say that you have had a wonderful career on Wall Street and that you are most well regarded by your peers. We find no reason to be concerned with either you or your wife's personal life. Hopefully the questions that we put to you and the answers you give us will provide us with some insight in regards to what you saw in Berlin the days up to and including the time when Hitler invaded Poland. In a few moments The President will be joining us as he is most interested, as we are, in your remarks.

Chris's thoughts were mainly about his meeting the President face to face and what should he say to him and should he offer to shake his hand or just to wave at him. He was a bit nervous. A side door opened and there was Mr. Roosevelt being wheeled into the room and placed at the opposite side of the table. Chris was not surprised that he was in a wheel chair as he knew he had been crippled as a youth with polio. Mr. Cashman went to him and whispered something in his ear. The President, with a huge smile on his face, looked directly at Chris and said "Mr. Casey. Welcome to The White House. I trust that you have been treated well since your arrival in Washington. We are all very interested in the events that had taken place upon your arrival in Berlin with your wife and the events that took place with your exit from Germany by way of Madrid. Please be comfortable and if there is anything you need please let us know" Chris stuttered his response saying "Mr. President. I hope I can be of some help to you."

He began to tell his story as best he could from the moment they arrived in Berlin up to and including his departure from Berlin and then from Madrid. He was interrupted a number of times with questions from the group. "What was the response by the Germans when they were told about the invasion of Poland". He replied" There was dancing and cheering everywhere. It was like the whole city was celebrating the event. This celebration seemed to continue all of the days I was in Berlin both day and night. Soldiers and civilians alike joined in the celebration. It was an amazing picture. I was told by a German who spoke English that the Germans had bought into all the things that Adolph Hitler had talked about in his lengthy speech to the Reichstag regarding the new Germany". In response to the question regarding what we saw at the Jewish Synagogues in Berlin Chris said" The few Jews, who were on the trip with us, asked the German guide about why the Synagogues were all torn down?" He answered "Hitler was building brand new synagogues for them but they had not been finished yet". "I don't think that anyone on the tour believed what they were being told about the synagogues". He was asked how the group had been treated after the announcement of the invasion. He said "We were all scared especially the Jews in our group. We saw that our German guide was most excited and pleased with the news of the invasion. When we returned to the hotel, the guide was no where to be found and he had all of our passports. Since we had seen and heard many things about what was going on in Germany we were afraid that we would not be allowed to leave Berlin to tell the world what we had seen and heard. The guide had all this information about each of us and there was no doubt that he would pass that information along. My wife and I agreed that we needed to find a way to get back home so we enlisted the help of a Spanish citizen who I have referred to in my previous accounts".

CHAPTER TWENTY-ONE

The questions continued and he did the best he could to answer them. Of course, they were most interested in the whereabouts of his wife and how Hitler and Franco were involved in their escape from Germany. After a while Mr. Cashman said "Thank you for your cooperation. You need to make yourself available to us in the days ahead as we might have need to get some additional information. You will be provided with a hotel room for the night and we will be happy to pay for your meals while you are in Washington. In addition if you would send me a note showing the cost of airfare, we will reimburse you. You are welcome to have breakfast at the hotel in the morning and sign the check with your hotel room number. After your breakfast, we will drive you to the airport and you may board your return flight back home. Again, on behalf of the President, we thank you for your testimony and wish you a safe passage home. On your arrival at Newark, you will be met by one of my associates and driven to your home." President Roosevelt nodded his head and mouthed "Thank you. Mr. Casey".

On his way back to the hotel in Washington, Chris thought about the meeting he just left. He did not seem at all surprised with the questions he was asked. He did wonder whether anything he told them would be helpful. He felt he was treated with the respect he deserved as CEO of his Bank. Mr. Foxworthy accompanied him back to the hotel and, just before pulling up to the hotel entrance, Foxworthy said to Chris "Do you want to talk to your kids this evening? I have their phone numbers at their Colleges so that once you are settled after your dinner, you can call them. I will leave their phone numbers with the hotel telephone operator and you can call the operator after your dinner and ask her to make the call a conference call." This brightened his spirit but he struggled with what he would tell them about Pat even though Pat had been in touch with them.

After having dinner it was about 7:30 This would be a good time to talk with Sam and Laura as they are probably in their dorm rooms. The hotel operator said she would call him back once the call had been created. He was anxious but happy that they would talk in a few minutes. When the phone rang both of the kids began to talk at the same time so he said "Laura, you go first and by the way it is so good to hear your voices". In an anxious voice Laura said" Both of us were so shocked when Mom called to tell us that she would be staying in Europe for an extended period of time. She tried to explain it but we did not understand. How are you and when are you coming home? When can we see you so that you can fill us in on what the heck is going on.". He asked them if they could make it home after classes on Friday and then they would have the rest of the weekend to visit. They said that would work for them. He finished the call saying "I look forward to seeing you on Friday and did they need any money etc." They said that all was ok money wise so he told them he loved them and said goodbye. Sleep came early for him. The alarm rang at 7AM and he dressed and waited to hear from Mr. Foxworthy. Shortly there came a knock on the door and they went to the dining room for breakfast.

There was little conversation as they were about enjoying the meal and they left the restaurant at 8:30 walking to the same car from last night. The driver asked where his luggage was and he laughed and told him that all he had was his shaving gear and toothbrush in this bag. Upon arrival at the airport they went out on the tarmac where a US Army plane was parked. Walking up the staircase, Chris thanked Mr. Foxworthy, entered the plane and took the first seat he reached. He hoped his trip home would be comfortable and that he was excited to soon see his kids.

It was a short flight to Newark. He was met there and driven to his home. As they approached his home, he felt both happiness to be back home and yet unhappy that Pat was not with him. In some ways it felt like a hollow moment. The house would be empty except for him.

He needed to change the clothes he had been wearing since Madrid, take a shower and shave using his own razor. It felt good to get used to being home although without Pat he was not overjoyed.

Escape from Berlin

The mail had piled up in the entry way so he quickly went through it and kept only the bills which he needed to pay. It seemed like he was trying to do a lot of tasks to keep from worrying about what had happened in Germany and in Spain. He would be seeing the kids in few days so he did have something to look forward to.

He knew there would be lots of questions from them but resolved to be positive with his answers. He called his secretary at the Bank and told her he was home and would be at the office early in the morning. She reminded him that there was a Board meeting on Thursday where he would assume the CEO position and she would help him prepare for it. As he hung up he decided not to share any of the sordid details of his trip to Germany but just to say that Pat was spending a bit more time in Spain.

Since they had been gone for a while he needed to go to the market to replenish the food supply so he made a list, picked up what he needed and returned home. Good thing he had asked his neighbor to start his car from time to time so that the battery would be ok. Since he had eaten breakfast, he made himself a sandwich and got ready for bed. The phone rang and it startled him. Pat was on the phone asking if he was ok and did he have a safe trip home. She went on to say" How is the house? Is everything ok there? Have you talked to the children?" He replied" Everything is ok here. No problems with the house except it is not the same without you. Please, please tell me that you are coming home. I am miserable without you. I talked to the kids and they will be home this Friday for the weekend so I need to be ready to talk with them. It would be great if I could tell them that you would be home in a matter of days.". Her response was that she needed more time and he needed to be patient with her. Before she hung up she said that she loved him and that she would keep in touch.

The tears started and he really had a good cry but he needed to be patient as she had asked. What else could he do? He turned on the radio to hear the war news. Most of the news was about England and France declaring war on Germany on Sept 3rd 1939. They did this in support of Poland. There was no mention of any military action by them so far. The question raised by the commentator was when would the US become involved in the conflict. He said there were two schools of thought here at home. The first was that we need not be involved again in a war in Europe especially since the English and French were involved while the other school talked about the inevitability of our involvement. Of course the longer that Pat stayed in Spain, the more her safety was in doubt.

Over the next few days he attended to his new responsibilities at work which included the Board meeting. They offered their congratulations to their new CEO and that they would be supportive anyway they could. While at work, a few of his colleagues called to welcome him home, ask about the vacation and to wish him luck. This support network felt really good to him and for a bit he was able to take his mind off his problems. The good news was that the war in Europe had not been a major problem for the Bank but he knew they had to prepare for that changing so he asked his secretary to call his Senior Staff to invite them to a meeting in the main conference room on Monday morning at 8 and that it was important for everyone to attend. He spent a bit of time checking on the markets. It was clear that there was great concern on the Street.

CHAPTER TWENTY-TWO

It was early Friday afternoon and he decided to leave work early as the kids would be home in a matter of hours. His plan was, of course was to welcome them home and then to invite them out to their favorite Italian Restaurant where they could talk about their Mom. Shortly after returning home first Laura and then Sam arrived. They greeted each other with lots of hugs and kisses. Chris asked them to settle in their rooms and then come downstairs so they could talk. He had 5,000 butterflies in his stomach as he waited for them in the family room.

Sam was much more laid back than his sister so the conversation began with Susan asking him what the heck was going on. Be positive Chris thought so he began by saying "I talked to Mom last night when she called to make sure I was home safely. I know you guys have had at least one conversation with her over the past few days. Rather than continue on, I have made a reservation for dinner at Villa Deste as I know you guys love their food and we can talk in a very relaxed environment." They agreed and they went on their way in his car.

After they had ordered their food, Chris said "I know you are anxious for me to share with you what, as you said, the heck is going on. I want to be honest with you so here goes. I don't know what your Mom said but I will start at the beginning".

After giving them almost a blow by blow story of all that had happened after their arrival in Berlin, he waited to let them ask the questions that they needed for him to answer. In the meantime their food had arrived. While listening to his story, the kids only picked at their food and Chris did not lift his fork. His hope for relaxation did not turn out the way he wanted either for him or the kids. The questions they had were all about Mom, Juan Carlos and about their relationship. Chris tried his best to soft sell what he thought by saying, You guys probably never heard the expression "midlife crisis" unless you heard it from me or from Mom. It happens to both men and women alike who are in their 40's and 50's. It occurs out of the blue at times when all is going well in a person's life. Little things in one's life can trigger this affliction creating a need to embrace a way of life that, up until then, was never even considered. I believe that this is the place in life where Mom is. For me I am naturally upset about this and I know you are too but, like many unpleasant things that will come about in your life, you need to put yourself in God's hands and let Him take care of it. It will require lots of prayers for your Mom but for the three of us, it will require patience. Mom has told us that she will keep in touch with us as time goes on so, even if we don't fully understand, we need to give her time to sort this out. In the meantime we need to be strong for each other and continue our lives as normally as we can.".

He felt physically and emotionally drained after he finished. All three of them had tears in their eyes which was to be expected. He asked them to please try and enjoy the dinner and then they would go home and try and digest all of this and they will resume the conversation in the morning. He told them that he loved them and that all would be ok even though he was not sure that it would be. They hugged and kissed as the they made they're to their bedrooms.

CHAPTER TWENTY-THREE

It was Saturday and Chris decided to get up early so he would be available to the kids when they woke up. He had been up for several hours and he did not hear any sounds coming from their bedrooms so he made himself some coffee, read the newspaper that was delivered every day and decided to use the time to pay the bills that had stacked up during the trip. It helped take his mind off things. After a bit he was getting a little anxious about what the kids were doing so he went up to their rooms and the rooms were empty. He could see that the beds were slept in but no kids. He began to be a bit panicky. Coming back down he noticed that Laura's car was not outside. Trying to regain his composure, he thought that they probably gotten up earlier and drove somewhere to talk about all that went on last night.

He was right. It was not too much longer that the kids came driving up and came in. They told him exactly what he had thought. "We wanted to be away from the house to talk about last night. For both of us it was hard to hear about Mom but we hashed over what you said about letting God take charge. From our earliest recollection you and Mom always talked about how God was in charge and that we would always be ok. And so, even though this is hard for us, we will do as you ask but we are most concerned about you"

Sam voiced with obvious conviction with Laura periodically nodding her head. Sam continued, "Will you be ok when we leave tomorrow to go back to school? How will you manage without Mom? What can we do to be of help and supportive?"

Chris answered them "I will be ok. You know that I have been given a huge responsibility at the Bank so many folks are depending on me so my plate will be full with lots to do. Let's plan to talk on the phone at least once a week and you guys need to do your thing at school. I will let you know when I hear from Mom and you do the same."

The rest of the day on Saturday was spent by the kids connecting with friends who might be home from college for the weekend. Chris asked them to be home no later than 6pm because he was going to bring in food from the local Chinese restaurant. They agreed and went on their way. Chris puttered around the house and, at 5:30, went to buy dinner. When he returned they were both there. Not much conversation during dinner and they all went to bed rather early as the kids wanted to get up and leave early to go back to school. And so it was as the leaves were beginning to turn in mid September of 1939.

CHAPTER TWENTY-FOUR

On September 17th 1939 Canada declared war on Germany and the battle of the Atlantic began.

On September 17th the Soviet Union invaded Poland.

In early October Adolph Hitler ordered the euthanasia of the sick and the wounded which he described as those whose lives were unworthy of living.

An excerpt from Hitler's speech to the Reichstag on October 6th, 1939.

"As Fuehrer of the German people and Chancellor of the Reich, I can thank God at this moment that he has so wonderfully blessed us in our hard struggle for what is our right, and beg Him that we and all other nations may find the right way, so that not only the German people but all Europe may once more be granted the blessing of peace."

On this day German and Soviet forces gained complete control over Poland and began to divide the country between them. Germany annexed Western Poland and Danzig and the Russians began the Sovietization of their newly acquired part of Poland.

On October 14th German troops are on the French border. It was rumored that Germany might make one more peace offer to France before attacking.

In late November 1939, The Soviet Union attacked Finland but their progress was slow.

On December 30th, 1939 Hitler told the German people that 1940 would be the most decisive year in German History.

On February 11th 1940 President Roosevelt sent Sumner Wells to Europe on a mission to meet with the leaders of the great powers: France and Great Britain.

On March 12th, 1940 Finland signed a peace treaty with The Soviet Union.

On April 9th Germany invaded Denmark and Norway.

On May 10th 1940 Germany invaded France, Belgium, Luxembourg and the Netherlands.

On May 15th, 1940 the Netherlands surrendered to Germany. It was thought at that time that the United States was not properly prepared to defend Europe.

On May 26th 1940 during the battle of France the British Forces were cut off from the French army and had to make a retreat back to England from the port of Dunkirk leaving behind most of their heavy equipment. It took over 900 boats to evacuate the Allied Forces.

On June 4th the Germans bombed Paris and on June 10th Norway surrenders to Germany and Italy declared war on England and France

On June 14th German forces entered Paris. More importantly on this date Spanish troops occupied Tangier in Morocco. Franco offered Hitler a Spanish entry into the war if Hitler would agree to allow Spain to control all of French Morocco, parts of Algeria, and an expansion of Spanish Guinea. Hitler would not accept those terms, but in October, Hitler and Franco met and plans were made for a joint campaign against Gibraltar.

Later that month the Soviets began their occupation of the Baltic. On June 22, 1940 France signed an armistice with Germany. Shortly thereafter German subs began attacking Allied merchant shipping in the Atlantic.

July 3rd the Germans launched a major air attack on England. In Amsterdam all Jews were required to register

Escape from Berlin

July 10th The Germans attacked British shipping over the Channel. The Battle for Britain had begun.

August 3rd. Italy occupied British Somaliland in Africa.

August 17 Germany declared a blockade of Britain. In a few days the air raids on London begin

August 31st President Roosevelt called up 60,000 National Guards

September 3,1940. Roosevelt announced the Lend Lease Program giving England 50 destroyers in return for US air bases in the Caribbean.

September 7, 1940. 400 German bombers and 600 fighters targeted docks in England. Germany warned that all ships in war zones are subject to attack regardless of nationality.

September 16th. First peace time draft in US history

September 27. Japan allied itself with Italy and Germany

October 7th. Germans invaded Romania

October 28. Italy invaded Greece and Britain occupied Crete.

November 23. Hungary and Romania joined the Axis

December 9. Britain began an offensive in Africa. In early January Tobruk in Africa fell to England.

March 7th. Britain landed in Greece.

April 1941. US began to patrol the Atlantic. Germany invaded Greece and Yugoslavia who quickly surrender to Germany.

May 1941. German attack on Tobruk is repulsed. Britain counter attacked in Egypt. British ship Hood is sunk by the Bismark and shortly thereafter Britain sunk the Bismark.

In June of 1941 Germany invaded Russia and Franco

identified himself with the German cause. Franco sent 100,000 workers to Germany to help with the war production. Spain also obtained a neutral position toward Britain and the US and Russia decided not to declare war on Spain. Thousands of Spanish refugees crossed the country to get to Lisbon Portgugal and then, for some, crossing the Atlantic to the US. This was significant as you will see later on.

CHAPTER TWENTY-FIVE

Over the next few years from late 1939 through mid 1941 the US Stock markets were down each year. This was an especially difficult time for financial institutions in the United States. Chris had many problems to deal with during this period of time in his role as CEO of the Bank. Client confidence was at a very low point although not as bad as in 1929. The Board was very supportive of his decision making during these times. The war in Europe and the real possibility that the US would become involved created much angst on the Street. The two sides, the hawks and the doves, were constantly attacking each other which led to much concern by the average citizen. In addition some of the hawkish moves by the President fueled the fire of the isolationists. He had just begun his 3rd term in 1941 and the world was virtually in chaos. The war in Europe was not going well for the Allies so the pressure on the US to enter the war was magnified.

Remembering back to the fall of 1939, Chris had just taken over as CEO. His kids were on their way back to college after hearing about their Mom and her decision to stay in Europe. For the children and himself they were well aware of the dangers that Pat faced the longer she stayed in Spain. It was very difficult for all of them. Pat did call them every once and a while but, while they pleaded with her to come home, she was steadfast in her choice to remain in Spain.

During the next few years Chris mulled over the possibility of Pat never coming back to the US. His thoughts were around seeking a divorce. Although he never let on to the kids what he was thinking, time and hope were fading. He was still a relatively young man and had most of his life ahead of him. If the US went to war he knew that he was a bit too old to be drafted or even to enlist. It was not long before folks began to realize that Pat was not coming home. At this point he had to tell everyone the truth about her plans. Most friends and relatives were dumbfounded with her choice to stay in Spain and her relationship with Juan Carlos. Most were very supportive of him and the kids in the months leading up to the summer of 1941.

With the notion that there was no way for the US to stay out of the war, many college students and recent graduates were enlisting by the thousands. Sam graduated from college in May of 1941. He was 21 at the time and very much an adult with his own personal beliefs. He felt that there would be a war so he enlisted in the U.S. Army Air Force shortly after graduation. Sam came home and he explained his decision to his dad and to Laura. Chris was not happy about Sam's decision but was not about to be critical of his choice. Both Laura and Chris expressed their concerns for the danger he was facing but they both sent him on his way to the Air Force training field where Sam would be stationed and trained...

They had not heard from Pat for several weeks and they had no way to contact her as she was very secretive about her location over the past few years. Of course, the events in Spain (as addressed in the preceding chapter) were worrisome, as this is where they believed Pat was living. Their concern for Pat's safety was magnified by the current news from Europe.

Chris was able, through the Banks contacts in Spain, to ask for help in locating Pat. He supplied them with all the information he had about her and about Juan Carlos's position in the Spanish Government. There was little to no feedback from their sources in Spain which made Chris more uncomfortable.

Again he managed to continue to prioritize his position with his Bank. The strong possibility that Japan would enter the war as an Axis power seemed very real and this added to the fears on the Street and with the general public. Laura had accepted a teaching position at a grade school in Summit. She seemed happy and they hardly ever talked about Pat in the Fall of 1941. She was living at home with Chris which was a big comfort for him to have her there. By this time Sam had completed his pilot training and came home for a brief visit. He told them that he was being sent to US Army Air Force base in Texas where he would learn to fly the B17 which was the strategic bomber in the Air Force. He had been commissioned a 1st Lieutenant and wore his uniform with great passion. No question that he would be very much involved in the coming conflict which would certainly include the US and its military forces.

CHAPTER TWENTY-SIX

Over the past few years, from time to time, Chris thought about the visit he had at the White House with the President and his people several years ago.. He often wondered why he never received any calls from Mr. Foxworthy or from anyone else in Washington. As CEO of the Bank he often testified to one or more Congressional committees, having been summoned to the Capital but that was the extent of his interfacing with the Capital crowd. However, in September of 1941 he received a phone call at the Bank from an official at the War Department in DC. He was asked to fly to Washington the next day and come to the War Office building. He asked the gentleman why he had to come and his answer was he could not discuss it over the phone. So, the next day he flew to the Capital and, with the directions he was given, he took a taxi to the War Office Building.

The security was very heavy at the War Office. He was frisked and questioned by the Marines once inside. After he was cleared he was escorted to a corner office on the 6th floor. Entering he was greeted by a civilian (He thought he could tell the difference between Military folks and civilians). He learned that military folks sometimes wore civilian clothes. He was directed to follow him into a large office. Seated behind the huge desk, amazingly, was Mr. Foxworthy. He was a bit older and had put on some weight but it was him. Foxworthy motioned for him to be seated in a sofa while he sat next to him in an easy chair. "So good to see you again Mr. Casey. It has been a while and a lot has gone on in the world since we last met. No doubt you are wondering why I sent for you. Well, hold onto your seat tightly and listen to what I have to say. There is no way you would know this but we have been keeping tabs on your wife during her time in Spain. Our intelligence system has long arms all over the world. We have been especially mindful of the part that Franco has been playing in world events. Since your wife's friend Don Carlos is an important player in Spain, we needed to keep an eye on him and his associates which would include your wife. We have learned nothing which would lead us to believe that your wife was involved politically in Europe. Quite the contrary. She has been a model US citizen what we would call an expatriate. It has come to our attention that your wife has fled Spain along with a great number of others and escaped, and are now in neutral Portugal. She is now safe in the US consulate in Lisbon and we are in the process of bringing her back home."

WOW. Did Chris just hear that Pat was coming home? "When will she be here? Is she Ok? Is she coming home willingly Did she have any message for me and the kids? he said. Foxworthy answered "She is ok and is coming home willingly. However, when she arrives in Washington, we will need to debrief her in a similar but more extensive way than we did with you some years ago. So, it may be as long as a week before we can release her so you can stay here or go home. If home is your choice, we will call you when we are finished with her and then you may return here to see her and hopefully go home. She has sent her love and apology to you and your children and is looking forward to being with you. Before you leave my office, please let me know what choice you have made. If you wish to stay we will book a hotel room for you and pay for all your expenditures while you are here in Washington".

Chris was so excited never dreaming of this ending after so long a time almost 2 years. He asked Foxworthy if he could call Laura and let her know the news. He was provided with a private office and a phone. Chris told him he would make the choice of staying or going home after he talked to his daughter. He did not know how to get in touch with Sam so he hoped Laura might know.

Chris tried to reach Laura but she was busy teaching at her school. He left a message saying that he would call later in the evening. He asked if he could put him up at a hotel and he would be talking to Laura this evening. After eating dinner at the Hotel dinning room he went back to his room and called the hotel operator and asked her to make the call to Laura. Needless to say she was overjoyed with the news about her Mom and asked all kinds of questions. He told her that the Government would let him know when he could come back to Washington to meet Mom and that he would call her so she could meet them at home. She knew how to reach Sam so she promised to call him and give him the news.

Chris was given a phone number to call to let Foxworthy know what his plans were. The message he left said that he would be returning home in the morning. When Mr. Foxworthy was ready to send Pat home, please call him at work or at home giving him the phone numbers.

Chris was back in his office by noon the next day and told everyone he could that Pat was finally coming home. Questions were asked but not answered by him except to say that he was thrilled with the news. Over the next few days he spoke to Laura and to Sam a number of times as they were both anxious for any news. It was not until the following Monday that Mr. Foxworthy called to say that Pat was ready to come home and would he come to Washington the next day to greet her and bring her home.

Chris repeated the trip that he had taken almost 10 days ago to the War Office in Washington where he was led back to Mr. Foxworthy's office. The minute the door was opened he saw Pat sitting in a chair across from Mr. Foxworthy. She turned and saw Chris and they both ran towards each other and hugged. They both took a step backwards and took a long look at each other and then hugged again. They started to speak to each other at the same time which created laughter from both of them. Chris said "You first." but she shook her head no so he spoke" It is just unreal to be with you after all this time. I have prayed every day that this time would come. I know this will be difficult for both of us as we get to know each other again but time is on our side. I have let Sam and Laura know that we are on our way home so they will be there to greet us." She starred right into his eyes, hugged him and said" Let's go home"

www.ingramcontent.com/pod-product-compliance
Lightning Source LLC
LaVergne TN
LVHW051953060526
838201LV00059B/3620